CLARENCE E. MACARTNEY

12 Great Questions About Christ

Other Books by Clarence E. Macartney

Twelve Great Questions About Christ

Great Women of the Bible

Paul the Man

The Greatest Texts of the Bible

He Chose Twelve

Clarence E. Macartney

12 Great Questions About Christ

Grand Rapids, MI 49501

To
My Mother
Clear in mind, strong in faith,
Great in love.

Twelve Great Questions About Christ, by Clarence Edward Macartney, © 1993 by Kregel Publications, P.O. Box 2607, Grand Rapids, Michigan, 49501.

Cover and Book Design: Alan G. Hartman

Library of Congress Cataloging-in-Publication Data

Macartney, Clarence Edward Noble, 1879-1957.
Twelve great questions about Christ / Clarence Edward Macartney.
p. cm.
Originally published: New York : Flemming H. Revell, 1923.
1. Jesus Christ—Person and offices—Sermons.
2. Presbyterian Church—United States—Sermons.
3. Sermons, American. I. Title.
BT201.M18 1992 232—dc20 92-23990
CIP

ISBN 0-8254-3267-7

1 2 3 4 5 year / printing 97 96 95 94 93

Printed in the United States of America

CONTENTS

FOREWORD

The title of this book may cause misgiving in certain quarters. "Questions about Christ" are sometimes thought to be unnecessary; we may differ in our opinions about Christ, it is said, and yet have Christ Himself; we may trust Him without taking sides in theological controversies. But a little reflection shows the absurdity of such indifferentism. Faith in a person always involves opinions about the person in whom faith is reposed; it is impossible to trust a person whom one holds to be untrustworthy. So it is in the case of our relation to Christ. It is really preposterous to place "theology" in contrast to simple faith; for the "theological" questions which are being debated in the Church today are not questions which lie on the periphery of Christian belief, but concern rather the central question whether Jesus was merely a prophet who initiated a new type of religious life or a Savior to whom we may safely commit the destinies of the soul.

It is these great matters which are discussed in this book. They are discussed by a preacher of proven power, and in the book the secret of his power is revealed. Dr. Macartney is a preacher because he has a message—a message which it is reasonable to accept. He is not engaged merely in voicing his own opinions on the subjects of religion or ethics or sociology; but when he comes forth into the pulpit he comes from a secret place of meditation and power, and with the message which God has given him to proclaim. The center and core of the message is Jesus Christ—not the reduced and unreal Jesus of modern naturalistic Liberalism, but the all-sufficient Savior presented in the Word of God. But may we still hold to the Jesus of the Word of God? That is the real question which is being faced by the Church today. And it is convincingly answered in the twelve chapters of the present book.

J. Gresham Machen, D.D.

Late Professor of New Testament Literature aud Exegesis
Princeton Theological Seminary (1916-29)
Westminster Theological Seminary (1929-37)

1

Was Christ Born of the Virgin Mary?

The Holy Ghost shall come upon thee, and the power of the Highest shall overshadow thee: therefore also that holy thing which shall be born of thee shall be called the Son of God (Luke 1:35).

From the beginning, the Christian Church held the doctrine of the supernatural conception and Virgin Birth of Jesus Christ to be a true and essential portion of the faith once delivered unto the saints. To unbelief in all of its forms this doctrine has always been offensive. As early as the third century we find the opponents of Christianity centering their attack upon the narratives of the Virgin Birth, and from age to age, men who hate the Christian religion and wish that it were driven out of the world have bitterly assailed this doctrine of catholic Christianity. There is therefore nothing strange in the present day revival of the ancient assaults upon the Virgin Birth. The only new and strange thing about this old enmity is the kind of men who make the attack. Formerly, it was made by non-Christians and anti-Christians—men outside the Church. But now we find men in the Church saying of the Virgin Birth of our Lord practically what Ingersoll, Haeckel, Paine, Voltaire, Celsus and Cerinthus said. Many declare that the credibility and significance of Christianity are in no way affected by the doctrine of the Virgin Birth, and some go so far as to say that the doctrine is a stumbling block to faith, and puts a barrier between Jesus and the race, and that narratives of the Virgin Birth in the Gospels arose in much the same way as the old legends and myths about the supernatural births of famous personages of the pagan world.

That such utterances as these should be made by men inside the Christian Church, and by men solemnly ordained to proclaim to the world the Gospel of Christ, shows the necessity of reaffirming the doctrine of the manner of the Incarnation, and reviewing those impregnable grounds upon which the Church has received and held this truth for so many ages.

In discussing this article of Christianity let us remember that we are dealing with a great mystery. The beginning of all life is a mystery, over which science, which can tell us so much about the progress and change of things, has shed not even the feeblest ray of light. Pondering the mystery of his own birth and existence the Psalmist said, "I will praise thee for I am fearfully and wonderfully made; marvelous are thy works and that my soul knoweth right well. My substance was not hid from thee when I was made in secret and curiously wrought in the lowest parts of the earth. Thine eye did see my substance yet being imperfect, and in thy book all my members were written which in continuance were fashioned, when as yet there were none of them." If this be true of the birth and conception of man, how much more of the conception and the birth of the God-man Jesus Christ! "Great is the mystery of godliness," says St. Paul, and he goes on to define wherein the mystery consists: It is the mystery of the Incarnation: God manifest in the flesh.

In discussing the doctrine of the Virgin Birth we shall, for the sake of clearness and simplicity, divide the subject into two parts. First, the fact of the Virgin Birth, and secondly, the meaning of the fact, or the place of the fact in Christian faith.

The Fact of the Virgin Birth

The doctrine of the Virgin Birth is, ultimately, a question of fact. Those who depart from historic Christianity at this point cannot with any degree of plausibility claim, as they do in regard to other doctrines of the Christian faith, that they differ only as to interpretation, for this is not a matter of theory and interpretation, but a matter of fact. Was Christ, or was He not, born of the Virgin Mary? From the very beginning the Church has believed that the birth of Christ was "on this wise," namely, that He was born of the Virgin Mary. No one disputes the antiquity or the universality of this belief. The question before us now is, How did such a belief arise? Was it a carefully fabricated legend, or myth, cleverly foisted upon the intelligence and faith of the first disciples? Was it a story put into the Gospels by some interpolator, long after the original manuscripts were written? Did it come, as we are told many good Christians believe it did come, from a natural desire on the part of the believers in Jesus to account for His manifest uniqueness and superiority of character, in other words, as the myths about Plato and Augustus and Hercules arose? Or, did the belief in the Virgin Birth originate in the *fact* of the Virgin Birth? The Christian Church holds that it was the fact of the Virgin Birth which gave rise to the belief in the Virgin Birth. What evidence have we for the fact?

The evidence upon which we base our faith in the Virgin Birth is the narratives of the Gospels. There are four Gospels, but only two of them, Matthew and Luke, tell anything about the birth of Jesus. Mark commences with the Baptism of Jesus by John, as does also John, after a prologue in which he states the fact of the Incarnation but tells us nothing as to the manner. But both Matthew and Luke, in plain and yet beautiful language, tell us of the Virgin Birth of Jesus. Their accounts are evidently independent narratives, yet not in conflict, and in many respects they complement one another.

Take, first, the record of Matthew. He tells us that there was a man named Joseph who was about to take as his wife a maiden named Mary. Before the marriage, he discovered that Mary was about to become a mother. Joseph had only one explanation of such a condition, namely, that Mary had been faithless to the vows of her espousal. Of course, he could not proceed with the marriage under these circumstances, but instead of heralding her shame before the townsfolk of Nazareth, and publicly humiliating her, Joseph, who was "a just man," was deliberating as to how he might put her away in some private manner. He was in the midst of his meditations when there appeared unto him the angel of the Lord.

The angel told him not to hesitate about proceeding to marry Mary, for she had not been faithless to the law of purity, but "that which is conceived in her is of the Holy Ghost." She would soon give birth to a son whose name would be Jesus (Savior) for He would save His people from their sins. Moreover, all this was in fulfillment of an ancient prophecy of Isaiah that a virgin should give birth to a son, and the name of the son should be Immanuel (God with us). After this interview with the angel, Joseph took Mary as his wife, and shortly thereafter Mary gave birth to Jesus at Bethlehem.

Such is the story of Matthew. Turn now to the story of Luke. Luke tells us that the angel Gabriel came to visit a virgin named Mary, at Nazareth, who was espoused to a man named Joseph, of the house of David, and said to her, "Hail, thou that art highly favored, the Lord is with thee." The virgin was confused and frightened upon hearing such a greeting, but the angel proceeded to make clear the reason for it by telling her that she would shortly give birth to a son whose name would be Jesus, and that this son would have the throne of David and would reign forever. Then Mary asked a very natural and simple question: "How can I give birth to a son, when I am not even married?" In answer to this the angel said that without a husband and through the agency of the Holy Spirit she would give birth to the child: "The Holy Ghost shall come upon thee, and the power of the Highest shall overshadow thee: Therefore also shall that holy thing which shall be born of thee be called the Son of God." Then follows the lovely narrative of how Mary and Joseph went up to Bethlehem to be taxed, and there in a manger, "because there was no room for them in the inn," Mary gave birth to the Savior of the world.

Such, in brief, are the narratives of the birth of Christ. They are found in documents which, by common consent, go back to the Apostolic age, at least to the first century. Leaving aside all theories as to inspiration, these two men, Matthew and Luke, are, on the face of the Gospels they wrote, serious-minded men, sensible, earnest and honest. One of them, Luke, because in a subsequent book, the book of the Acts, he touches upon a great deal of the geography and politics of the Roman world, stands out as one of the most reliable historians the world has ever known.

In the introduction to this Gospel, just before he relates the birth of Jesus, Luke tells us that he has made every effort to get from the original sources the facts about Jesus which he relates. Those who deny, or are indifferent to, the Virgin Birth have made much of the silence of the other two Gospels, Mark and John, on the subject. That silence, in its place, I will hereafter discuss. But how much these contemners of the Virgin Birth must have wished that for their purposes of denial or discounting it had been the great historian Luke who was silent on the subject, instead of the fragmentary Mark or the philosophical John.

These narratives are in the Gospels of Matthew and Luke as we possess them. But, the question will be asked, Do they deserve to be there? Do the most ancient manuscripts of the New Testament contain them? Our revised English Bible did not, of course, drop down from heaven just as we possess it. It is a translation made by devout scholars based upon a study and comparison of the oldest documents of the New Testament. The original autographs of the Gospels are lost. The nearest we can come to them is through the ancient manuscripts. The text of our Bible is built up on the authority of the manuscripts. For example, one will see in the margin of a copy of Mark's Gospel a statement that the last verses of the Gospel are absent from many ancient manuscripts. And in John's Gospel one will see that the story of Christ and the woman taken in adultery is bracketed, with the statement that these verses are not found in many of the ancient manuscripts.

It would greatly strengthen the case of those who wish to reject the Virgin Birth if it should be discovered that the Birth narratives of Matthew and Luke are lacking from many of the ancient manuscripts of the New Testament. But upon appealing to those manuscripts, what do we find? We find that there is not a single unmutilated manuscript of the New Testament which does not contain the Birth narratives. The same is true of the ancient versions of the New Testament, or the translation from the Greek into the popular tongues of the different countries. Every manuscript and every version bears witness that the Birth narratives are genuine sections of the two Gospels in which they are found, and furthermore, as Wiess says, "there never were forms of Matthew or Luke without the Infancy narratives."

Confronted by the overwhelming evidence of the manuscripts, the enemies of the Virgin Birth next try to discredit the narratives by saying that these sections which tell of the Virgin Birth, although found in the oldest manuscripts of the Gospels, were probably not parts of the original Gospels, but are additions, or interpolations. There is not the slightest evidence of this, and all efforts to disintegrate the integrity of the Birth narratives have failed completely. There is nothing to favor it, except the disinclinations of these men to believe such a thing. The Virgin Birth ought not to have happened; according to their naturalistic theories, it did not happen; therefore, these verses which say it did happen must be the work of the interpolator. But their clever manipulations, dropping out a verse here and a clause there, are all palpably inadequate. The verses which tell of the Virgin Birth are as much a part of the original narratives as the old foundations under a church rebuilt are a part of the original building. Moreover, supposing for a moment that some interpolator had tampered with the original documents and grafted on to them the stories of the Virgin Birth, why then did he not complete his work by striking out the two tables of genealogy which have ever been a difficulty in the way of accepting the Virgin Birth? If a fabricator added these verses to gain credence for the Virgin Birth, surely he never would have allowed the tables of genealogy to stand as they are.

Unable to discredit the Birth narratives on the ground of their non-genuineness or non-integrity, the enemies of the doctrine bring up objections. So first of all, they mention what I have just adverted to, the two tables of genealogy. Two problems are involved in these tables, one, the apparent discrepancy between that of Matthew and Luke. That is a matter which does not bear on our present subject. But the second problem does. It is that these tables seem to give the genealogy or descent of Jesus, not through Mary, but through Joseph. This is not the place to go into the detail of these tables. All that we need to show now is, that the very men who put these tables in their Gospels, Matthew and Luke, are the men who tell of the supernatural birth of Christ, and yet are conscious of no contradiction between those narratives which say Jesus was born of the Virgin Mary, and the tables which seem to trace His descent through Joseph. More than that, not only are they conscious of no contradiction, but they are careful in writing these tables not to say that Joseph was the father of Jesus.

Matthew employs a periphrasis saying, "And Jacob begat Joseph the husband of Mary, of whom—the feminine pronoun—was born Jesus who is called Christ," whereas Luke says, "Jesus began to be about thirty years of age, being as was supposed, the son of Joseph, which was the son of Heli."

Again, attention is called to statements in these Gospels where Jesus is referred to as the son of Joseph; for example, "the carpenter's son"; "Jesus of Nazareth, the son of Joseph"; "Joseph's son." And how else could these people of Bethlehem, Nazareth, Capernaum, and elsewhere, have spoken of Jesus? The people knew no differently, and to all outward appearances Joseph was the father of Jesus. It is not strange that they thus referred to Jesus. The strange thing would have been if they had thought of Jesus as other than the son of Joseph. But what of the other references, not by the people at large, but by Luke himself, where three times he speaks of "his parents," and where Mary herself said to Jesus, "Thy father and I have sought thee sorrowing"? Luke is conscious of no conflict in thus referring to Joseph as the father of Jesus. To the people Jesus was only Joseph's son. Thus the two evangelists reflect the popular thought of Jesus in relationship to Joseph and Mary, and at the same time gives the true information about His supernatural birth. Here they speak of Jesus as Joseph's son, as outwardly He was; and here they tell of how He was conceived by the Holy Spirit and born of the Virgin Mary. Only a man who did not wish to receive the doctrine would ever have thought this double reference strange, or that it pointed to fabrication and fraud.

Another objection brought against the doctrine of the Virgin Birth is the silence of other portions of the New Testament. Mark's Gospel is silent on the subject, also John, so also Paul. In the book of the Acts, where we have a record of the first preaching of Christ to the world by the apostles, there is no reference to the Virgin Birth. Because of this it is held that the authority of the narratives in Matthew and Luke is broken down, for, we are told, it is inconceivable that if these other writers knew of the Virgin Birth they would have kept silent about it. But is it? Let us see.

The argument *ex silentio* is generally an unsound one, never more so than in this instance. Mark says nothing about a Virgin Birth of Christ. Granted. But what of it? Neither does he speak of the birth of Christ in any form whatever. Would you infer from that silence that therefore Jesus never was born, never came into the world at all? Certainly not. Where does Mark's Gospel begin? With the Baptism of Jesus, or the public life and ministry of Jesus. The fact that he does not write about the birth and childhood of Jesus in no way invalidates the facts related by Matthew and Luke, any more than McMasters, in his history of the United States, which commences with the year 1784, invalidates the facts about the colonial history of the United States which are related by Bancroft. You might as well argue that there was no Declaration of Independence and no Bunker Hill because there is no mention of these events in a history of the United States which commenced with the Civil War, as to argue that there was no Virgin Birth because Mark, who records the public life of Jesus, makes no reference to it. The birth and childhood of Jesus lay outside the scope and plan of his treatise.

But what about John? Since his Gospel comes latest, well along in the apostolic age, no one can think that John could have been ignorant of the fact of the Virgin Birth, or of the traditions and narratives which dealt with the supposed fact. He must have been familiar with the writings of Matthew and Luke. He must have known all that there was to know, for it was into his keeping that Jesus, on the Cross, committed His mother for maintenance and filial affection. If Jesus were born of the Virgin, it is inconceivable that John should not have known of it. Again, if these were only idle tales, and thus reflecting on the honor of Christ and of Mary, would John have kept silence? But he did keep silence. He did not say a word to repudiate the statements of Luke and Matthew, and the only rational interpretation of that silence is that since he does not deny or repudiate the Virgin Birth, he accepts it and takes it for granted.

Although John does not directly refer to the Virgin Birth, in his sublime prologue stating only the fact of the Incarnation, that the Word became flesh, his narrative agrees with the Virgin Birth. John, not less than men today, must have asked himself about the manner of the coming of this tremendous personality, the God-Man of his Gospel, into the world. All others must be born again, not of flesh, nor the will of man, but of the will of God. But if Jesus escaped that universal necessity of regeneration, upon what ground was it? It must have been because he did not share by natural generation the sinful stain of our fallen nature. The point of the argument is that the Christ of John's Gospel is such a person, such a character, as cannot be accounted for in any natural way. The miracle of the Virgin Birth does account for Him, and since John not only does not repudiate that teaching of Luke and Matthew, but has many utterances about Christ which beautifully agree with the narrative of the Virgin Birth, the reasonable inference is that he did know of the narratives of the Virgin Birth and accepted them because he knew them to be true.

There is an interesting tradition, too, about John once leaving the bath at Ephesus when the Gnostic heretic, Cerinthus, came in, because of his profound aversion for that heretic. One of the things which Cerinthus taught was the natural generation of Jesus with Joseph and Mary as His parents. The profound aversion of John for Cerinthus is unexplainable, if John, like Cerinthus, believed that Joseph was the father of Jesus; but it is perfectly clear if John knew and believed with his whole heart that the Word became flesh, being conceived by the Holy Spirit and born of the Virgin Mary.

A case parallel with John's account of the coming of Christ is his account of the advent of John the Baptist. Luke gives in considerable detail the story of the birth of the Baptist, just as he does the birth of Jesus, telling us of John's parents, Zacharias and Elizabeth, and the angel's annunciation. But all that John says of the coming of John the Baptist is that "there was a man sent from God whose name was John." Yet who would argue from this silence of John that he had never heard of Zacharias and Elizabeth? One would have as good reason for saying that John had never heard of the circumstances of John the Baptist's birth because in telling of John's coming he says nothing about them, as for believing that he knew nothing of the Virgin Birth because he makes no definite reference to it in telling of the advent of Jesus Christ.

The next silence with which we must deal, and which is brought up against the doctrine of the Virgin Birth, is that of St. Paul. Let it be granted that there is no definite statement of the Virgin Birth in Paul's writings, though this is far from what a recent writer says when he describes deniers of the Virgin Birth comforting themselves with the assurance that they have given up nothing vital in Christian faith because they remember that John and Paul do not even "distantly allude" to it. In his convincing book on the Virgin Birth, Dr. James Orr points out the indisputable fact that Paul, in speaking of the Incarnation of Christ, always employed "some significant peculiarity of expression" such as "God sending His Son" (Rom. 1:3; 5:12); "becoming in the likeness of men" (Philippians 2:7); and the unusual Greek form in Galatians 4:4, "born of a woman." In view of this, to say that Paul does not even "distantly allude" to the Virgin Birth is a rather sweeping claim, a peculiar example of that backhanded dogmatism with which the rationalists are always reproaching men who accept the facts of the New Testament as facts.

Paul hardly ever refers to the incidents of Christ's earthly life, save His death, and what immediately preceded it, the Lord's Supper. The Resurrection is the great confirmatory miracle with which Paul deals. But his intimate knowledge of the facts of the Resurrection, as well as the institution of the Lord's Supper, indicates a full knowledge of the facts of Christ's life. It would have been strange, indeed, if this great initial fact in the life of Jesus was never told to Paul by any of the disciples with whom he talked, or by Luke himself, who was the traveling companion of Paul, and must have had some of the material for his Gospel in hand at that time. Moreover, aside from all definite references, Paul taught the universal guilt and sinfulness of man through inherited transgression. Yet Christ, without sin, comes to redeem sinners. Just as in the case of John, Paul's theology required a miracle of incarnation which would give Jesus a personality free from the corruption of original sin. The Virgin Birth supplies the miracle. I cannot conceive that Paul was ignorant of it. Certainly he does not repudiate it. On the contrary, such an expression as Galatians 4:4, "sent forth His Son, born of a woman," might well have come from the lips of a man who knew and believed the story of the Virgin Birth.

But even could it be proven (which, of course, it cannot) that neither John nor Paul even "distantly allude" to the Virgin Birth, that silence would be no warrant for rejecting the doctrine. Upon the same ground great portions of the New Testament narratives could be rejected. The Lord's Supper would have to go, because that disciple whom Jesus loved, and who on the last night at the

Passover Supper leaned upon His breast, in his Gospel tells nothing of the institution of the Lord's Supper. Likewise the Transfiguration must go, because of the four Gospels the only one written by one of the three disciples who went up the mount with Jesus, that of John, says nothing about it. So also the Ascension of Christ must be discarded because Matthew in his long and full narrative tells us nothing of the ascension of our Lord. The whole Christian tradition would disintegrate, did we apply this rule of the argument from silence.

The impregnable position held by the doctrine of the Virgin Birth in Christian literature and life is strikingly witnessed to by the complete unsatisfactoriness of the theories which would account for the presence of this belief and its record in the Christian literature upon some other hypothesis than that of historic fact. The tradition was present at a very early date in the Christian community. How did it arise, if not from the fact? Some have suggested that it came from Jewish sources. Disciples of Jesus believed that He was the Messiah, the Son of God, and therefore were ready to attribute to Him some miraculous entry in the world. Musing over the pages of the Old Testament, Matthew, or some other, came upon the prophecy in the seventh chapter of Isaiah, "Behold a virgin shall conceive and bear a son, and shall call his name Immanuel." Ready to ascribe any wonder to Christ, Matthew is said to have taken the suggestion of a Virgin Birth from the prophet, and fabricated a story that Jesus was so born, and put the tale into his Gospel, and after the same manner, Luke. In other words, the prophecy suggested the narrative of the Virgin Birth. But both Christian and Jewish scholars are agreed that this verse in Isaiah was never used with Messianic application before Christ was born, and that nowhere in Israel was there the expectation that the Christ was to be born of a virgin. The prophecy could not have suggested or inspired the narrative of the Virgin Birth, but it was the fact of the Virgin Birth which threw its illumination upon the prophecy.

Another favorite hypothesis has been that the Christian disciples tried to account for the preeminence of Jesus by applying to Him a myth of miraculous conception and birth after the manner of the pagans. A popular preacher has well stated this hypothesis in one of his sermons:

"To believe in Virgin Birth as an explanation of great personality," he says, "is one of the familiar ways in which the ancient world was accustomed to account for unusual superiority. Many people suppose that only once in history do we run across a record of supernatural birth. Upon the contrary, stories of miraculous generation are among the commonest traditions of antiquity. Especially is this true about the founders of great religions. According to the records of their faiths, Buddha and Zoroaster and Lao-Tsze and Mahavira were all supernaturally born. Moses, Confucius and Mohammed are the only great founders of religions in history to whom miraculous birth is not attributed. That is to say, when a personality arose so high that men adored him, the ancient world attributed his superiority to some special divine influence in his generation, and they commonly phrased their faith in terms of miraculous birth. So Pythagoras was called virgin born, and Plato, and Augustus Caesar, and many more.

"Knowing this, there are within the evangelical churches large groups of people whose opinion about our Lord's coming would run as follows: those first disciples adored Jesus—as we do; when they thought about His coming, they were sure that He came specially from God—as we are; this adoration and conviction they associated with God's special influence and intention in His birth—as we do; but they phrased it in terms of a biological miracle that our modern minds cannot use. So far from thinking that they have given up anything vital in the New Testament's attitude toward Jesus, these Christians remember that the two men who contributed most to the Church's thought of the divine meaning of the Christ were Paul and John, who never even distantly allude to the Virgin Birth."

Let us see what this implies. In the case of Augustus the myth was that his mother, asleep in the temple of Apollo, had been visited by that god in the shape of a serpent, and the fruit of this miscegenation was Octavius, afterwards Augustus. In any collection of classic myths there will be found numerous accounts of the liasons of the gods with mortal women—how Alcempe, for example, the daughter of Electryon, was beloved by Jupiter. The result of their union was Hercules. But Juno, fiercely jealous of her lord's mortal children, sent two great serpents to destroy Hercules as he lay in his cradle, but the precocious youth strangled them with his hands.

What these old myths tell of is lust-inflamed gods who visit women on earth and beget children after a carnal manner.

In his article on Virgin Birth in Hastings' *Encyclopedia of Religion and Ethics*, J. A. MacCalloch points out that in the case of Buddha actual physical generation through father and mother is implied in his birth-tales, and in the case of Zoroaster physical generation is related. Supernatural elements are added, but as Dr. MacCulloch clearly points out, there is no ground whatever for saying that the stories of the birth of Zoroaster and Buddha are comparable to the New Testament account of the Virgin Birth. And as for tales of great men begotten by serpents, or of libidinous pagan gods having children by mortal women, between such tales and the narratives of the Virgin Birth of our Lord there is a gulf fixed. Tertullian intimates that difference where he says, "God's own Son was born, but not so born as to make Him ashamed of the name of Son or of His paternal origin. It was not His lot to have as His father, by incest with a sister, or by violation of a daughter, or another's wife, a god in the shape of a serpent, or ox, or bird, or lover, for vile ends transforming himself into the gold of Danaus. These are your divinities upon whom these base deeds of Jupiter were done."

When anyone tells us of these superior Christians—"some of the best Christian life and consecration of this generation, multitudes of men and women, devout and reverent Christians"—who conceive of the doctrine of the Virgin Birth as created in the same way in which the tales about great pagan personalities or the fabulous heroes of antiquity were invented, the reply of Origen to Celsus is still to the point, "Since Celsus has introduced the Jew disputing with Jesus, and tearing in pieces, as he imagines, the fiction of His birth from a Virgin, comparing the Greek fables about Danae, and Melanippe, and Auge, and Antiope, our answer is that such language becomes a buffoon and not one who is writing in a serious tone." Perhaps in the whole history of anti-Christian propaganda nothing so preposterous has ever been suggested as that the early Christian community, so intensely prejudiced against the pagan thought and custom—so much so that rather than conform to it they would give up life itself—borrowed from the pagans the myth of the Virgin Birth and accounted for their Savior and Redeemer after the manner of the heathen.

Where, then, did this story of the Virgin Birth arise? It could not have come from Jewish sources, neither could it have been borrowed from the Gentile world. Where did it come from? It came from the fact. The only explanation of the belief, received and defended by the whole Church, is that Christ, as the narrative tells us, was conceived by the Holy Spirit and born of the Virgin Mary.

The Meaning of the Fact

We hear it frequently said, today, that, accepted or rejected, the Virgin Birth does not in any vital way affect Christian faith and doctrine. Such a view certainly has not been that of the foes of Christianity who, from age to age, have directed their assault upon this article of the Christian creed. Nor can such a view be held in reality by those within the Church today, who speak lightly of the Virgin Birth, for one of their chief arguments against it is the argument *ex silentio*, namely, that if true, such a doctrine would never have been left out of the other two Gospels or the writings of Paul, which means that the doctrine, out of the mouth of its critics, is a most important one. In their conflicts with Judaism and heathenism the early Church constantly appealed to the Virgin Birth as witnessing to the full humanity, and also the deity and the sinlessness of Christ. Certainly the force of the argument is not less needed today than it was in the days of Gnostics and Docetists and Ebionites.

The Virgin Birth, although strangely neglected and overlooked in the modern literature of evidences and apologetics, just as miracles and prophecy are, witnesses to the following truths about Jesus Christ:

1. *The Historical Reality of His Person.* Any man's life and personality consists of a series of facts, where he was born, and of whom, where he has lived and what he has done, and where and when he died and was buried. The earthly life of Jesus is not otherwise. It is made up of a series of facts, and only those facts give us any condition of the Person of Christ. Just as all that we see of a building rests upon its foundations, so the great Personality of Christ rests upon the facts of His earthly life. This fact of the

Virgin Birth is the initial fact of the earthly life of our Lord, it is one of that series of facts which, taken together, present to us the glorious Person, Jesus Christ. We have no Christ but the Christ of those facts. Since this is true, this fact of the Virgin Birth, the initial fact of His life, is an essential fact. If it goes, all that follows goes. The only Christ we know is the Christ of the New Testament, and that Christ was born of the Virgin Mary. That fact about Him is as carefully attested as any other fact of His life. Therefore, the denial of it involves the denial of Christ, for it permits, in turn, the denial of any other fact of the life of Christ.

2. *The Virgin Birth witnesses to the Deity of Christ.* Here and there we hear a voice which says that the deity of Christ is not involved in the question of the Virgin Birth, and that a man can still cling to the deity of our Lord although he rejects His Virgin Birth Theoretically, this might seem true; but as a matter of fact the vast majority of those who reject the Virgin Birth deny also the deity of Christ. One follows the other in natural and logical sequence. Early cherished beliefs, and a loyalty to Christ which is the heritage handed down from believing men and women who received all the New Testament facts about Christ may keep a man from plunging into that pit of darkness and despair which go with a denial that Jesus was the Son of God. But has the world ever yet seen a man who denied the Virgin Birth who either did not fall in that abyss or totter in peril on its brink? Whatever new theology may think of the doctrinal bearing of the Virgin Birth, the most direct witness to the deity of Christ found anywhere in the Bible bases that deity upon the Virgin Birth, for so the Angel said to Mary: "The Holy Ghost shall come upon thee, and the power of the Highest shall overshadow thee: THEREFORE also that holy thing which shall be born of thee shall be called the Son of God."

Dr. Charles Briggs, in his article "Criticism and Dogma," published many years ago in "The North American Review," thus witnesses to the place of the Virgin Birth in Christian faith:

"The philosophical difficulties which beset the doctrine of the Virgin Birth do not concern the Virgin Birth in particular, but the Incarnation in general. Indeed, the doctrine of the Virgin Birth seems to be the only way of overcoming the chief difficulties. If the pre-existent Son of God became incarnate by ordinary generation, we could not escape the conclusion that a human individual person was begotten. The Incarnation would then not be a real Incarnation, but an inhabitation of Jesus by the Son of God, with two distinct personalities, that of the pre-existent Son of God and that of the begotten son of Joseph. . . . The man Jesus would be a prophet, a hero, a great exemplar, but not the Savior of mankind. He might be the last and greatest of the heroes of Faith, but not God Incarnate. Only a God-man who had taken human nature into organic union with Himself and so identified Himself with the human race as to become the common man, the second Adam, the head of the race, could redeem the race. The doctrine of the Virgin Birth gives such a God-man. Natural generation could not possibly give us such a God-man. Therefore, the doctrine of the Virgin Birth is essential to the integrity of the Incarnation, as the Incarnation is to the doctrine of Christ and Christian Salvation."

Dr. Briggs then states that while the Virgin Birth is essential to the faith of the Church he does not feel that it is essential to the faith or Christian life of individuals. "The doctrine may for various reasons be so difficult for them that they cannot honestly accept it." He seems to make a distinction between what the Church can tolerate and what it can endorse. Yet he fully grants, and ably demonstrates, the essential place which the Virgin Birth holds in Christian faith: "For it is a dogma which is inextricably involved in the Christological principle that lies at the basis of Christian Dogma and Christian Institutions. They cannot possibly recognize that the birth of Christ was by ordinary human generation, for that would be a revival of the Nestorian heresy and be a denial of all the Christian Philosophy of the centuries, with all the serious consequences therein involved. It would turn back the dial of Christianity nearly two thousand years; it would break with Historical Christianity and its apostolic foundation, and imperil Christianity itself."

3. *The Virgin Birth witnesses to the sinlessness, the holiness of Christ,* and to all the hopes of humanity which rest upon that sinlessness. God created one sinless man, sinless, though free to fall. That first man, created in God's image, fell, and after him all men have sinned and fallen. Generation after generation, race after race, people after people, and nation after nation, under all conditions

and circumstances, yet always the same monotonous result, a sinful man, a corrupt human nature. Then, according to our Christian faith, God sent forth a new creation, a second Adam, the preexistent and eternal Son of God, manifest in the flesh, assuming human nature, not fallen and stained and corrupted human nature, but human nature as God created it in the beginning, in the image of God. Again the great experiment is to be tried, while men and angels and devils look on with breathless interest. Will the second Adam fall like the first? Will temptation bring His forehead, too, down to the dust? The result of that experiment is the record of the Gospels. Christ kept perfectly the law of God, and by virtue of that perfect obedience demonstrated and won His right to be our Redeemer and to make satisfaction for our sins.

All the rivers of Christian theology become one great life-giving stream in the Cross of Christ. But if Jesus were the son of Joseph and Mary, then He was not free from the taint of sin, He was not separate from sinners. You have left in that manger-cradle at Bethlehem the Child who may become a world's great prophet, leader, dreamer, reformer, but Jesus, the Savior, the Redeemer, is gone! Christ is lost to humanity! Wise men of the East, take back your gifts which you have laid at His cradled feet, for the child is not the King of Heaven and Earth. Shepherds, standing in silent awe in the lowly cavern where the young child lies, go back to your sheep upon the fields, for this world and its cares are the only reality! Angels, whose music comes floating down from heaven's gates, silence your sweet songs and leave mankind to the grim music of its sobs and moans and curses and blasphemies. Star of Bethlehem, tender dayspring from on high, go out and leave this world in the blackness of darkness, forever groping in endless cycles with its lusts and its illusions, for Jesus is not that Holy thing which shall be called the Son of God, and shall save us from our sins. He was born of flesh and of the will of man, not of the will of God. Our Christ is gone, and with Him dies the hope of humanity.

2

DID CHRIST FULFILL PROPHECY?

And beginning at Moses and all the prophets he expounded to them in all the Scriptures the things concerning Himself (Luke 24:27).

The minds of men are differently constituted. To one mind one kind of evidence appeals more strongly than another. The remarkable thing about the Christian religion is that it carries with it all kinds of evidence to suit all kinds of minds. One appreciates this when one begins to enumerate the different proofs of the Christian faith. There is the adaptation of Christianity to the needs of human nature, how deep calls unto deep. There is its rapid spread in the world by purely moral means; its congruity with all the true and beautiful that man has conceived of before Christ or since Christ; the effect of Christianity upon the lives of its professors; the perfection of Christian ideals and morality; the character of Jesus; the miracles of Jesus; the two great miracles certificatory of His Divine Sonship, the Virgin Birth and the Resurrection from the dead; and last in this catalogue of enumeration, but always first in the New Testament and in the teaching of Jesus and the preaching of His apostles, the fulfillment of the ancient prophecies. Any kind of evidence that a reasonable mind could ask for, Christianity has to present. God has made the way of unbelief the most difficult of all roads for man to travel. He has hedged it up with barrier after barrier, so that before a man can become, or remain an infidel, he must believe moral impossibilities.

We are now to consider just one of the proofs of the Christian religion, the fulfillment by Jesus Christ of the ancient prophecies. This is an argument which appeals with equal power to believers and unbelievers. It is the one great evidence to which the Bible itself points. It is the argument of Christ about Himself. It is the one great argument of the apostles for the authority of Jesus Christ.

THE PROOF OF PROPHECY

What is the argument from prophecy, and how does it apply to Jesus Christ? The answer is, that if we have a series of predictions foretelling clearly and closely future events which no native shrewdness and no clever guess could have arrived at, and the fulfillment of which could not have been cleverly contrived by an impostor, then the fulfillment of these predictions necessitates a supernatural power at work. In other words, the fulfillment of prophecy proves that Christianity is a divine revelation. "To declare a thing shall come to pass long before it is in being, and then to bring it to pass, this or nothing, is the work of God" (Justin Martyr). As applied to Christ, the argument resolves itself into this: Did Christ in His life and death, and the influences which flow from His ministry, fulfil the prophecies made in the Old Testament? If He did, then He must be the Son of God and the world's Savior.

In this connection let us remember that, although long and tender usage has made the word "Christ" part of the personal name of Jesus, it is in reality not a name, but a title. It is the Greek word which means "the anointed one." The Hebrew form of the word is "Messiah," which also means "anointed," and was the name applied by the Jews to the great king, priest, and prophet for whose coming they had been looking for long centuries. Jesus Christ really means, then, Jesus the Christ, or the Messiah spoken of in the Old Testament.

Was Jesus really that Christ? That was the wonder in the mind of the woman of Samaria when, after Jesus had talked with her and had searched the chambers of her heart with His truth, she said to her townsfolk: "Come, see a man which told me all things that ever I did: is not this the Christ?" One of the first disciples of Jesus, Andrew, said to his brother Peter when he asked him to come and talk with Jesus, "We have found the Messias, which is, being interpreted, the Christ." Upon the correctness of that opinion that Jesus was the Christ, Christianity stands or falls. There is no such thing as separating the New Testament from the Old Testament, or taking the precepts and the ideals of Jesus apart from His claims, and this greatest of all claims that He was the Christ, the Son of the Blessed; for if He were not the Christ, then He was either an ignorant man, or a bad man for claiming to be the Christ.

The first disciples followed Jesus because they believed He was the Messiah, the Christ. The Jews put Jesus to death because He claimed to be the Christ. The disciples of Jesus preached His Gospel everywhere in the world because they believed Him to be the Christ. Thus our discussion is doubly important, for not only is Christ fulfilling prophecy, which is the great argument for the truth of Christianity, but, on the other hand, if Christ did not fulfil prophecy, then Christianity is condemned.

This great evidence is peculiar to Christianity. No other religion hazards an appeal to the fulfillment of prophecy. Christianity accepts this greatest of tests. If some centuries before Christ some one man had uttered predictions of the coming of one like unto Christ, and these predictions had been fulfilled, that, in itself, would be of infinite importance. But instead of one man at one time in history uttering a prediction which has been fulfilled, we have many predictions uttered by many different men through many hundreds of years, and all at last converging in Jesus Christ. "A whole people announce Him and subsist during four thousand years in order to render as a body testimony of the assurances which they have of Him, and from which they can be turned by no menaces and no persecutions." It is not strange, then, that the fine mind of Pascal saw in the fulfillment the strongest of all the evidences for Christianity, the one which takes in all others, for he said: "The greatest of the proofs of Jesus Christ are the prophecies. They are also what God has most provided for, for the event which has fulfilled them is a miracle which has subsisted from the birth of Christ even to the end."

Nahum and Nineveh

Why, it may be asked, do we pay such attention to the prophecies of the Old Testament? For the reason that we are compelled to do so. Regardless of the prophecies which refer to Christ, there are many predictions in the Old Testament which have been strikingly fulfilled. For instance, many of the predictions uttered by the prophets concern the great contemporary nations which surrounded Israel and warred against her. One of the greatest of these peoples was the Assyrians, with their capital at Nineveh on the Tigris. In a passage of great eloquence the prophet Nahum predicts the siege of Nineveh; how the chariots would rage in her highways, the scarlet uniforms flash in the streets, and the cypress spears be brandished. We can hear the rumble of the wheels, the crack of the whips, and behold the dismal heaps of the slain, the spoiling of the temples and the palaces. When the Medes took and destroyed Nineveh they were aided by a sudden rise of the Tigris, which swept away a part of the City's wall. Even this seems to have been predicted by Nahum, for he says, "The gates of the rivers are opened, and the palace is dissolved." So completely was Nineveh destroyed, and so utterly did it sink beneath the horizon of antiquity that even in classical times it became a myth, and in his Anabasis, Xenophon tells us how Cyrus and his ten thousand Greeks camped near some vast ruins which they supposed to be Nineveh. It was not until 1845 that the very site of Nineveh was rediscovered by the spade of the archeologist. I cite this one instance of a strikingly fulfilled prophecy to show how any prediction which we find in the Old Testament deserves to be taken seriously.

Prophecy Fulfilled in the New Testament

We turn now to a different class of predictions in the Old Testament—those which relate to the Christ, the Messiah. We cannot avoid these predictions even if we would, for they confront us, not merely in the pages of the Old Testament, but in the pages of the New Testament as well. Over and over again, the Gospels, particularly the Gospel of Matthew, tells us that this or that fact in the life of Jesus was in fulfillment of prophecy—"that the Scriptures might be fulfilled," is the refrain which sounds everywhere in the New Testament. Not only did these men believe that Christ was fulfilling the prophecies, but Christ, Himself, believed that He was, and said that He was.

"Search the Scriptures," said He, "for these are they which

testify of me"; "Moses wrote of me"; "The Son of Man goeth as it was written of Him." When He walked with the two disciples on the road to Emmaus on the day of the Resurrection, and wished to prove to them His identity, that He was really that Jesus whom they had known in the flesh, He did not work any miracle for them, nor appeal to some of His great sayings with which they might be familiar and thus confirm His personality, but He took them back into the Old Testament and said, "O fools, and slow of heart to believe all that the prophets have spoken: Ought not Christ to have suffered these things and to have entered into his glory? And beginning at Moses and all the prophets, he expounded unto them in all the scriptures the things concerning himself." Again, when Jesus was on trial before the council of the Jews, and even by perjury and slander they could not get sufficient evidence to convict Him, the high priest put Jesus on oath and said to Him, "I adjure thee by the living God that thou tell us whether thou art the Christ, the Son of God." And Jesus answered, "I am."

The same testimony to the fact that Jesus claimed to be the Christ is made by the apostles when they began to preach the Gospel to the world. They had little or nothing to say about the lovely character of Jesus, which seems to be the whole content of much modern preaching of the Gospel, but declared that His Incarnation and Death and Resurrection and Ascension and the bestowal by Him of the Holy Spirit were facts that had all been foretold centuries before by the prophets concerning the Christ, and that since Jesus fulfilled these prophecies He must be the Christ; publicly showing by the Scriptures that Jesus was Christ, and that therefore men must obey Him and believe in Him. As Peter put it in his great sermon, "To him, all prophets bear witness."

A Priest and Prophet Predicted

We have seen, then, that Jesus claimed that He fulfilled the Old Testament prophecies and that therefore He was the Christ, the Son of God. Now let us turn to these predictions of the Old Testament which Jesus claimed He fulfilled. At the very beginning of the Bible, we find that here is a book which is looking forward to a great event in the future. This series of promises for the future begins with the first announcement of the Gospel, that the Seed of the woman shall bruise the head of the serpent. To Abraham, in his day, it was predicted that in his seed, through his descendants, all the nations of the earth should be blessed. Moses, the great law-giver, assures the people that in the future God will raise up a great successor. Even prophets outside of Israel, under the Divine Spirit, foretell the coming of a mysterious Person, as when Balaam predicted on the mount of Moab: "I shall see him but not now: I shall behold him but not nigh. There shall come forth a star out of Jacob, and a scepter shall rise out of Israel."

The victorious reign of David and the peaceful reign of his successor, Solomon, serve as a foil to illustrate a greater King and Kingdom of the future—a King who is to have the heathen for His inheritance and the uttermost parts of the earth for His possession; who shall have dominion from sea to sea; whose Name shall endure forever, and in whom all men and all nations shall be blessed. The great prophets who speak at the period of the downfall of Israel and the captivity of her people, now begin to tell of a suffering and atoning servant, or Messiah, who shall, through death and suffering, lead the people to a state of happiness and glory, when peace shall be as lasting as the moon in the firmament, and the whole earth filled with the knowledge of the glory of the Lord. Now it is a king, and now a priest, and again a prophet who is predicted.

Together with these general and somewhat obscure predictions about a mysterious power and Person and blessing of the dim future, there is much that is more specific. This mysterious One is to be of the tribe of Judah, of the line of David; the place of his birth is to be Bethlehem Ephratah. "Out of thee shall he come forth unto me that is to the Ruler in Israel."

Not only the place but the time is specified, and specified so clearly that it was to be before the scepter finally departed from Judah, and while the Second Temple was still standing; His coming was to be preceded by the advent of a great prophet who should prepare His way by the proclamation of repentance and righteousness; He would work miracles, healing the sick and raising the dead; although He was a king, He would ride into Jerusalem, lowly, upon the foal of an ass; He would be rejected by His people; He would be sold for thirty pieces of silver; He would be mocked and reviled in the midst of His sufferings; gall and vinegar would be given Him to drink; His garments would be divided by lot; He would be pierced; He would be buried in a rich man's grave; although dead He would not be left in hades, nor would His body see corruption, and through the diffusion of His Gospel He would bring in everlasting righteousness.

WHO WAS PREDICTED?

No one who reads the Old Testament can doubt that all this is predicted of someone, and of some day in the future. The question is: Who is it that is thus described? Has He appeared in the world's history or is He yet to come? "Art thou He that should come, or look we for another?" Suppose that a man who had never heard of either the New Testament or Christ, has put into his hands a copy of the New Testament: What would such a man discover? He would discover that the great Person of the New Testament and His followers emphatically declare that this one Jesus is the One to whom the old predictions pointed, for they were fulfilled in Him. No man reading the New Testament could miss that claim. Then he begins to test the claims by the facts, and he discovers that Jesus was of the seed of a woman, of the seed of Abraham, of the tribe of Judah, of the house of David, that He was born while the Second Temple was still standing, that His birthplace was Bethlehem; that He did work miracles; that He was despised and rejected by men; that He was both a personage of strange unlimited powers, and yet of infinite humility and suffering; that He rode into Jerusalem on the foal of an ass; that He was betrayed and scourged and mocked and reviled, and that He was pierced; that men cast lots for His garments; that He was buried in a rich man's grave, and yet did not see corruption, for He rose again from the dead the third day. On comparing the Old Testament with the New, he discovers how one agrees with the other.

His observation would be: "This is a very striking thing, that so many conditions and actions predicted centuries before should be answered by the life and death of Jesus. If there were just one or two instances of a prediction having a fulfillment in Jesus, I should say it was a remarkable coincidence; but when I discover that over sixty things that are predicted of this mysterious, unknown personage in the Old Testament are similar to, or identical with, incidents in the history of Jesus of Nazareth, then I hardly know what to think."

Is it possible that there was collusion between Jesus and His friends, and that in order to gain prestige for His Gospel, through seeming to fulfil prophecy, Jesus contrived to make the incidents of His life and death fit into the predictions of the old prophets? This is preposterous, for most of the prophecies about Christ were fulfilled in His life and death by His enemies, who hated Him because He said He would fulfil prophecy and claimed to be the Christ.

Is it possible that some of these predictions were made after the event? No. The documents in which they occur, by common consent, long antedate Christianity. Is it possible, then, that although there are so many similarities between the historic life of Jesus and the things predicted in the prophets, the predictions really refer to some other man? If so, who is that other man? Socrates, Plato, Lycurgus, Alexander, Caesar Augustus, Tiberius, Justinian, Hadrian, Charlemague, Mohammed, Luther, Napoleon? Certainly not. In no person who can be named before Christ, or since His death, are there any incidents which fit into the Old Testament descriptions of the Messiah.

We are thus left to one of two conclusions: either the prophecies have not yet been fulfilled, or Christ fulfilled them. As to the former, what greater and fuller, more striking, fulfillment of the prophecies could be imagined than that which is afforded us in the life of Jesus Christ? Can you conceive of any figure arising in the future ages and giving greater evidence than Jesus did that He is the fulfillment of prophecy? It is impossible so to conceive. Taken by themselves, many of the predictions were inexplicable and apparently contradictory. How could He of whom they prophesied be a mighty conqueror, and at the same time despised and rejected of men? How could He be, at the same time, a priest, a prophet, and a king? Yet when Christ came, men saw how wonderfully all the ancient predictions converged and harmonized in Him. If Christ did not fulfil the prophecies, then they never will be fulfilled, for no greater proof of fulfillment could be offered than Christ has given us.

The only other conclusion is that Christ fulfilled the prophecies; that to Him all the prophets bear witness; that when Christ began at Moses and all the prophets and said Moses and the prophets were speaking of Him, He was not an impostor or a deceiver, but the Christ Himself, the Son of God.

What Does This Mean?

And what does this mean to us today? To those of us who already are Christians, believers in the Lord Jesus Christ, it means that our faith stands upon impregnable grounds. It means that when we come to church to worship, or when we kneel down at night by ourselves to pray for ourselves and for those whom we love, or when, in the hour of sorrow, we seek His comfort and help, or when the heart is heavy with the sense of sin and guilt, that the Jesus upon whom we call is the Christ, the Eternal Son of God, whose divine nature and whose right to save and to heal, to rule the hearts of men and rule the world has been demonstrated and vindicated by the mightiest evidence which could be presented to the mind of man. Since we say with Peter: "Thou art the Christ, the Son of God," therefore we can repeat his next sentence, "To whom shall we go? Thou hast the words of eternal life." He has the words of eternal life because He is the Christ, the Son of God.

For those who are not yet believers in Christ, this witness of prophecy has a very solemn meaning. It shows how and why unbelief is sin, and if persisted in, the unpardonable sin. Christ said: "He that believeth not, shall be condemned." Christ forgave the harlot and the extortioner; He forgave Peter who, with cruel oaths denied Him, and the thief on the cross stained with his crimes; but He cannot forgive the man who will not believe. He has given us the greatest reasons why we should believe and has put every obstacle in the way of unbelief.

Will you believe in Christ? I say, "Will you?" because it is an act of the will. Will you? Some of you have waited long, far too long. But Christ, with the marks of the nails in His hands and feet, God's eternal Son, wounded for your transgressions and bruised for your iniquities, still waits to be gracious unto you. Will you believe? To believe in Christ means to believe in all that is high and holy. It means to believe in God, in love, in justice, in life everlasting. Will you believe?

3

WAS JESUS AN ORIGINAL TEACHER?

Never man spake as this man (John 7:46).

This was the verdict of the officers whom the scribes and Pharisees at Jerusalem had sent out expressly to arrest Jesus. They returned without their prisoner, and when asked to explain their dereliction, answered: "Never man spake as this man." They could not lay their hands upon such a man.

A friend with whom I was having lunch once said to me: "How do you account for the efforts that are everywhere being made to discredit the Bible, and overthrow the authority of the Christian religion?" The answer is to be found in the mystery of iniquity, or the fact that the mind of man is alienated from God by sin, and one of the chief evidences of the fallen state of man is the effort which man makes to discredit the religion which comes to save him. The ways of doing this are ancient and innumerable, but the principle is always the same. The Bible commences with the declaration that "God said." But we have read only a few verses when we discover that the Tempter, speaking to the man and the woman, seeks to discredit what God said by asking this question:"Hath God said?" All forms of unbelief and resistance to the Christian faith are but repetitions of that first question and insinuation of the Tempter.

In recent years much has been made of the study of what is called

Comparative Religions. For people who have no axe to grind and no inveterate prejudice against the truth, such a study cannot be otherwise than helpful and confirmatory of the truth of the Christian revelation. But to others, it has seemed to furnish new weapons with which to assail the truth. In some ancient heathen cult, or religion, or philosophy, men have come across a sentiment which sounds like one of the sayings of Jesus; or they have read of some deed or incident in the lives of ancient prophets, or teachers, which is similar to an incident in the life of Jesus. There is nothing strange about that. The strange thing is the conclusion which they urge us to draw, the insinuation which they throw out, namely, that Christianity is not an original and separate and distinct religion, but some sort of an assembled religion, its precepts and practices a mosaic or patchwork of many other creeds. If true, this would, of course, destroy the authority of Christianity as a final and authoritative religion. We could no longer say that "there is no other Name given under heaven, among men, whereby we must be saved."

A Unique Teacher

Truth does not need to be new to be authoritative, and even if all the precepts of Jesus could be paralleled in some ancient faith, that would not make them any the less binding upon man, if they are true. But I will now try to show that Christ is not only a true teacher, but an absolutely original teacher, and that the verdict of the Hebrew officers: "Never man spake as this man," is a true verdict. This I shall do by showing that there never was such a speaker as Jesus; that is, "Never man spake as this man," for the simple reason that there never was another like Him.

But before coming to that main proposition, let me point out how even what is called the "ethical" teaching of Jesus, the Sermon on the Mount, for instance, is essentially new and original. Man everywhere and in all ages is a moral creature and has the same spiritual inheritance, however wrecked by sin and unenlightened by revelation he may be. Sin wrecked man's nature, but it did not destroy it. Therefore, any truth spoken in one age is applicable to man in every age, and truth spoken in one age will still be truth in every other age.

Man was created a moral being and sin has never stripped him of his moral nature. God never left Himself, as Paul said to the Athenians, without a witness. How true that is we know from the study of some of the heathen religions, for along with a great deal that is gross, revolting and false, we now and then come upon some great moral idea that is common to all men, and which Christianity could not improve on, for the simple reason that it is truth, unchanging truth. As an example of that take the case of the pagans who lived on the island of Malta, where Paul was shipwrecked. When they saw the serpent hanging on his arm they concluded that Paul was a murderer who, though he had escaped death in the shipwreck, yet justice suffered not to live. They were mistaken as to Paul, but not mistaken in their great belief that wrong doing will be punished. When Paul preached he could not deny nor change that fundamental conception, for back of his teaching that we must all stand before the judgment seat of God, and that whatsoever a man soweth, that also shall he reap, is the same great idea of the barbarians of Malta. Yet, related to Christ, what Paul taught was an immeasurable increase upon the knowledge of the barbarians of the island. It was new and original, for Paul preached a Christ who forgives the sinner.

TRUTH IS TRUTH

We are not to be frightened or surprised, therefore, if, in a saying of Plato, or Seneca, or Socrates, or Buddha, or an ancient Hebrew prophet, we discover a foregleam of the truth uttered by Jesus, or a faint adumbration of His perfect Law. We remember that He came to bring life and immortality to light, and what He said with regard to the Hebrew religion applies to any portion of truth uttered by the pagan and heathen faiths.

> "Children of men! the Unseen Power whose eye
> Forever doth accompany mankind,
> Hath looked on no religion scornfully
> That man did ever find.
> "Which has not taught weak wills how much they can?
> Which has not fallen on the dry heart like rain?
> Which has not cried to the sunk self-weary man;
> 'Thou must be born again'?"

All this we cheerfully grant. Still, even in this field of ethics, Jesus is an original teacher. There is such a thing as truth becoming cold and dead. Jesus made the dead live when He spoke. Those Jewish officers had undoubtedly heard the priests and Pharisees quote sayings of the great Rabbi Hillel or the older prophets of Israel, which were comparable to the words they heard from the lips of Jesus, yet their verdict was true, "Never man spake as this man."

Take, for example, Christ's law of forgiveness—"Love your enemies." It fell upon the world as something absolutely new and unique. Jesus spoke truly when He said to the disciples, "A new commandment I give unto you, that ye love one another." It matters not that some esoteric sage, talking to his little group, said something similar, or that some ancient faith intimated it; as a working principle of life it came new and fresh from Christ. As Sir John Seeley in his famous book *Ecce Homo* put it, "This is Christ's most striking innovation in morality. It has produced such an impression upon mankind that it is commonly regarded as the whole, or at least the fundamental part of the Christian moral system. When the Christian spirit is spoken of, it may be remarked that a forgiving spirit is usually meant. . . . To paraphrase the ancient Hebrew language, the Spirit of Christ brooded upon the face of the waters, and Christ said, Let there be forgiveness, and there was forgiveness."

Thus Christ was the first who made the world, as a world, take seriously a great law like that of forgiveness and the love of all men. When, then, I hear someone scoffing at Christianity because he says he has found what Jesus said in the sayings of Gautama, or Seneca, or Laotze, I am reminded of the story of that antiquarian who, after he had shown to a sculptor-friend how the characteristic features of Greek sculpture had been anticipated by the Egyptians, the Assyrians and the Hittites, exclaimed in triumph that the Greeks had invented nothing. To which his friend rejoined, "Nothing except the beautiful." The others had art, but the Greeks had art with beauty. Christ made the world take morality seriously, and if you wish to study comparative religions, do not buy a book on the subject, but buy a ticket and travel in those lands where the light of the Gospel has not penetrated.

But now to our main proposition that there never was such a teacher because there never was such a man.

1. *Jesus was an original teacher because He was a sinless man.* Men had heard about the truth before, but they had never seen a sinless man. Here was purity and love incarnate. All those great words had become flesh and dwelt among men. In contrast with other religions we at once relate the truth of Christianity to the character of the Founder of it. If, in the character of Jesus, there is the slightest taint, then down comes the whole Christian system, for it is involved with His personality. St. Paul said, "If any man love not the Lord Jesus Christ, let him he anathema maranatha." It would be absurd to condemn a man for not loving Gautama, Confucius, Plato, but if Jesus Christ be sinless—perfect—then, not to love the truth manifested is condemnation; Jesus Himself said that to His own generation. He called upon men to follow Him, and the imitation of Christ is the chief meditation and the chief labor of the Christian disciple. Jesus recognized the soundness of this test of His character as a witness to His teaching, for He said, "Which of you convinceth me of sin?" "If you can, then do not believe My words."

Strangers, like the two centurions, confessed to the moral miracle of Jesus, one saying, "I am not worthy that thou shouldst come under my roof," and the other exclaiming, "Surely this was the Son of God." His most intimate friends were under the same conviction. Peter, who fell at His feet and said, "Lord, depart from me for I am a sinful man," afterwards wrote of Him as a man, "Who did no sin, neither was guile found in his mouth." Then we have the testimony of men like Renan, Strauss, and others who spent much time and exhibited much ingenuity in trying to break down the Christian revelation, yet who all pay tribute to the moral supremacy of Christ. Even the charges brought against Jesus by His foes redound to His credit. He was charged with being a glutton because He ate with poor, outcast men. He was charged with breaking the Fourth Commandment because He healed on the Sabbath. They said He had a devil because He cast out the unclean spirits.

However you take Christ, in what are called the passive virtues—benevolence, compassion, humility, gentleness, patience, long-suffering, or in what are called the heroic virtues, fortitude, daring, courage, righteousness, indignation—it is as impossible to think of any improvement as it is impossible to conceive of any situation in life where He could not be your guide. To compare Him with others is not so much an offense against orthodoxy as it is against good taste and decency.

> "O what amiss may I forgive in thee,
> Jesus, good Paragon, thou Crystal Christ."

When such a man, therefore, talks to me of meekness, of purity, of forgiveness, of compassion, of reverence, I am confronted with an altogether new and original combination, for never before, nor elsewhere, have I heard the pure man talk of purity, or the all-forgiving of forgiveness, or the all-suffering of patience, or the all-pitiful of compassion. It is His personality, and that alone, which has persuaded men to seek first the Kingdom of God, or those virtues which Jesus commended to us. Jesus Himself is our moral dynamic.

2. *Because He identifies Himself with the truth which He teaches, Christ calls men to obey the commandments as He spiritually interpreted them, but still more does He call upon men to come to Himself.* "Come unto me," is the astounding invitation which He gives to men. Others have stood up before men and exhorted them to go in this direction or in that, or to receive this truth or that law; but Jesus tells men to come to Himself. "Come unto me." The refrain of the prophets is, "Thus saith the Lord," but Jesus says, "I say unto you." They asked men to take their message because it came from God. Jesus asked men to take Him because He came from God. Others have stood at the crossroads where pant and pass the weary sons of men on their pilgrimage through life, and they have called to them, "Here, this is the way"; "That is the truth"; "Yonder, you will find life." But the Galilean peasant stands at the crossroads and cries, "Come unto me all ye that labour and are heavy laden, and I will give you rest." "I am the way, I am the truth, I am the life."

Life After Death

The most striking example of how the supreme truth which Christ taught was Himself, is found in what He has to say about that problem over which the generations of men have bent in their sorrow and agony—life after death. Buddha knew nothing of life after death; the annihilation of the soul in Nirvana was the *summum bonum.* Divine revelation had not illuminated that territory to the devout Hebrew. Plato and Socrates and Cicero could speak and write in beautiful words about the reasonableness of it, and the desirableness of it. But when Christ came the world heard something that it had never heard before. He did not say, "There is a resurrection," "There must be a life after death," but, "I am the resurrection and the life. He that believeth in me shall never die!" All that we as Christians believe and hope for in the life to come is grounded upon the Person of Christ, that Person who could not see corruption, but was raised again from the dead, "declared to be the Son of God with power by the resurrection from the dead."

Thus the whole teaching of Jesus is identified with His Person. Can you think of Socrates taking the cup of hemlock and saying, "This cup is my blood which is shed for many for the remission of sins"? Can you think of any of the disciples of Plato saying, as a disciple of Jesus said of Him, "I am crucified with Plato, nevertheless I live, yet not I, but Plato liveth in me"? The question is so absurd, so grotesque, that it makes us aware of the gulf which yawns between Christ and all others. And that new life, which, we are told comes to the converted and reborn man, is not any principle of his own life, or any law which, adopted and obeyed, will carry him through to the goal of life, but Christ in him, the hope of glory. The whole meaning of the truth and the blessings of Christianity is realized for us, and summed up for us in Christ, and in our union with Him by faith. "For me, to live is Christ."

3. *The forgiveness of sin through His death is the grand, central, unique, and powerful thing in the teaching of Jesus.* Men have complained that if redemption by the Cross held the place in His mind which it has held in the mind of the Christian Church, He ought to have said more about it, and less about the sins of the Pharisees and the virtues of the meek and lowly. It is true that the full declaration and explanation of the sacrificial death and atoning blood of Christ comes after His death and from the lips of the apostles. But that is exactly what He provided for. He had to live and die before there was a Gospel to preach. When He had died

for our sins on the Cross, and had risen from the dead, then He sent the disciples forth to preach the Gospel unto every creature.

What is that Gospel? We know what the disciples who received the charge and commission took Jesus to mean. To them the Gospel meant the proclamation of the forgiveness of sins through faith in the Crucified Son of God. That was what they preached. That was what established the Church in the world. That is what kept the Church in the world. That, and that alone, will keep the Church in the world, Christ uplifted on the Cross, Christ bruised for our iniquities and wounded for our transgressions.

Where else will you find such a teacher? Where a teacher who makes such claims, who identifies himself with truth, who asks you to believe what He says for the tremendous reason, "I am God"? Is it a word of pity that you want to hear? Who will speak it so tenderly? Is it a word of hope that your sinking heart would like to hear? Who will speak with such conviction? Is it a word of comfort that you wish to hear? Who will speak so softly? Is it light that you want, rest that your soul craves, love that you covet and desire? Then where will you go but unto Christ? Is it the forgiveness of sin that your heart longs after, the blessed words of remission, the burden lifted, the stain washed out? Then where can you go but unto Christ? Lord, Lord, Lord, forsaken, forgotten, sinned against, neglected, scorned, crucified afresh by us all, O patient, divine Christ, O Son of Man, O Son of God, to whom shall we go but unto Thee? Thou hast the words of eternal life!

4

DID CHRIST WORK MIRACLES?

Jesus of Nazareth, a man approved of God unto you by miracles (Acts 2:22).

The two great pillars which support the temple of Christian truth and show it to be a revelation from God to man are the prophecies and the miracles. We have already spoken of the prophecies, which are in reality miracles of utterance. Now we come to those miracles of action which, according to the New Testament, were performed by Jesus Christ. We hear much today about the modern spirit of unbelief. There is no doubt about the unbelief, but there is nothing modern about it. It is as old as the mind of man. But there is perhaps more dogmatic denial of Christianity than there has been for many a day, and the most popular ground of the denial is what is called the scientific ground. The creed of this denial of Christ amounts to this: "Receive nothing you cannot demonstrate, and believe nothing you cannot see." Such a creed is neither scientific nor religious. It is but the manifestation of the pride of man's mind, the sin that made the angels fall, and which still keeps men from accepting the dominion of Jesus Christ.

It is because of the spread of physical science that not a few within the Christian Church have been tempted to deal lightly with the supernatural and miraculous element in the Christian revelation. Because physical science knows nothing of miracles, a great many Christians are almost afraid to say that their souls are their own, and they act as if they secretly wished that their New Testament did not have all these accounts of the prodigies which were done by Christ. Thus it has come about that what God gave to men as one of the two great evidences of the truth of the divinity and authority of Christ is mentioned almost with an apology by not a few writers and speakers in the Church. What the Savior Himself and His apostles pointed to as a proof and confirmation of Christian truth men today regard as sort of a stumbling block, an embarrassing addendum of Christianity, excess baggage, as it were, which they would like to be rid of. This is one of the many ways in which the Church, in order to gain favor with men and win their support, has come perilously near to a compromise with the world itself. No greater tragedy could befall the Christian Church than to have men think that Christians were ready to throw away any portion of the divine revelation for the sake of gaining the support of the mind of the age.

The quiet disregard, or the implied denial of certain great facts of the life of Christ as we have that life in the Bible, every rational mind must recognize to be, intellectually, absolute inconsistency. Christianity cannot be ethically divine and historically false. The man who is preaching the so-called ideals of the Christian faith and at the same time ignoring, or evading, or denying its facts, is indulging in a sort of theological legerdemain, which, if followed and adopted by others, could have no other result but complete denial of Christianity—ideals, facts, hopes, and all.

We want no soft, mossy bed of sentiment upon which to lie. We prefer the hard rock of fact, even though the facts cut and wound our pilgrim feet. Did Christ work these miracles attributed to Him in the Gospels? We know that the miracles are inextricably involved with the other facts of the life of Jesus, and that there is no Christ but the Christ who walked on the sea, and raised the dead, and made blind men to see. Men who talk about any other Christ are talking of a myth, a shadow, a vapor, for there can no more be a nonmiraculous, nonsupernatural Christianity than there can be a quadrangular circle.

The question which we face, then, the issue with which we are dealing, is a very great one—did Christ work miracles? This means not merely, did He feed five thousand men with five loaves and two fishes or did He raise the widow of Nain's son from the dead, or did He heal the paralytic at the Pool of Bethesda, but something far greater, namely, was there any such person as Christ at all? Has the world a divine Redeemer in whom it can trust? In answering our question, *Did Christ work miracles?* we shall speak first of the fact of the miracles, and second of their meaning and purpose.

THE FACT OF THE MIRACLES

We need waste no time in defining what a miracle is. I mean any of those prodigies which the Gospels say were done by Jesus, and which we know we cannot do ourselves and which could be done by no one of whom we have heard. Here is a short and adequate definition: "A miracle is an event occurring in the natural world, observed by the senses, produced by divine power, without any adequate human or natural cause, the purpose of which is to reveal the will of God and do good to man." That will describe any of the events in the Gospels which are commonly spoken of as miracles.

1. *Miracles are antecedently possible.* Dismiss, for a moment, the question about the historicity of the miracles related in the Gospels. There can be no doubt that such a thing as a miracle is a reasonable possibility, whether we ever saw one, or believed that other men had seen one, or not. Man knows what happens in his experience. Indeed, all so-called knowledge is but observation based upon a series of facts that have fallen within our observation. We cannot be dogmatic about what may have happened, or what can happen, beyond our field of observation. The Zulu chief would not believe it when his men told him that they had come back from England in an iron ship. Who ever heard of iron floating in the water? If, fifty years ago, a minister standing in a pulpit had made the prediction that within half a century one of his successors would stand in the same pulpit and preach, not only to the people gathered together in the church, but at the same time to people in New Jersey, Delaware, New York, and even as far away as New Hampshire and Wisconsin, that those people far off could hear and see the congregation sing the hymns—if he had said that, had predicted such a thing, his people would have thought him a

fit candidate for a madhouse. Yet that very thing, by means of radio and television, many preachers are doing any Sunday morning. Now the thing has come within the range of our observation, and we no longer marvel at it, even though we know very little how it is done. So we have to be careful about saying what can, or can not come to pass.

It is objected that a miracle is a violation of law, or God as He reveals Himself in nature. God, it is said, would contradict Himself if He did anything in another way. But this implies that we know all about God and His ways. Instead of that being so, how small a portion we have seen! The general uniformity of nature to which deniers of the miracles appeal is a blessing to man. It would be a terrible world in which to live if we could not count on the laws of gravity, of heat and cold, of summer and winter, seedtime and harvest. But this uniformity is consistent with voluntary control, and therefore for good and sufficient reasons, as the Bible tells us it has been, could be interrupted. When we speak of the uniform type of nature all we mean is that an effect is something produced by a cause, and that all the effects we see are produced by natural causes. But we have no right to conclude that therefore a miracle is impossible, for belief in miracles does not imply that an effect took place with no adequate cause, but that an effect was produced by the immediate act or will of God, who ordinarily works through second causes, but sometimes, if the Bible be true, through an immediate act. Instead of being a denial of the law of cause and effect, a miracle is its highest illustration.

A God who made a world and then shut Himself out from it so that He could never enter it again, never arrest, regulate, add to its laws of working, would be no God at all. He would be like a man who made a machine with whose laws of operation he could never interfere. What we call interference, arresting or changing of laws, may not really be such at all, but part of the great plan of God. To man it is a miracle, but not to God. If a counting machine produced, for millions of years, square numbers, and then, one day, produced a cube, it would be a miracle to the men who for generations had been using that machine, but not to the man who invented and so designed it that after so many square numbers had been produced it should bring forth a cube. Archbishop Trench tells how, in 1690, an agave plant was brought over and planted in the gardens of Hampton Court Palace by Queen Mary. The last ten years of the seventeenth century passed, and the plant gave no sign of flowering. The whole of the eighteenth century passed, and never a bud did the plant put forth. Eighty-eight years of the nineteenth century passed, and still no sign of a flower. But in 1889, the venerable plant burst into blossom. Several generations of men might have watched that plant and written learned books about it and said it was not of the flowering species, and that it could never blossom. "And yet they would have been wrong. The blossoming potency was there, latent, slumbering, deep-hidden in its core. It was no miracle, but a long delayed fulfillment of the law of its being, when it burst into blossom." The great miracle is God Himself. If you grant that, then all is possible.

> Admit a God—that mystery supreme!
> That cause uncaused! All other wonders cease:
> Nothing is marvelous for Him to do;
> Deny Him—all is mystery besides.

2. *A miracle is antecedently probable.* We have seen that if there is a God, there is a possibility of a miracle, if there should be need of one. We shall now see how a miracle is not only possible, but *probable*. The greatest question that we can ask is, Has God given a revelation of His will to man? God has created man with an ineradicable religious nature, a moral nature, which even in its perverted and degenerate forms bears witness to the grandeur and reality of the instinct itself. For God to make such a being and then never reveal Himself, never speak to that religious nature, would be like making the eye without light and the ear without sound. Still more would it be godlike in God to reveal Himself if this creation of His has gone astray and fallen a victim to its passions and its fears. Without a revelation, without a word from God, man has done nothing to clear away his darkness or break the chains of his slavery. If anywhere humanity has made progress, it is due to the fact that God has never abandoned the race, has never left Himself without a witness. Surely man needs a revelation. Has God revealed Himself? The destiny of a race hangs upon that question.

If, then, it is probable that a wise and beneficent God would reveal Himself, it is equally probable that there should be a miracle. How else could God authenticate a revelation? How, save by a miracle, would man in his fallen estate know that God had spoken to him? If by some great sign and wonder God had not said from age to age, "Lo, I am here!" how would man know that God was here, that God had spoken? It is the miracle, the departure from the observed uniformity of nature, that arrests the attention of man and makes him realize that a higher Person and a higher Power is at work. If that uniformity had never been broken, man would ever have been an atheist, he could never have known that God had spoken. But when the bush burns and is not consumed, when the ground is wet, but the fleece dry, or the fleece wet and the ground dry, or when the waves of the Red Sea are rolled back, or when, in a night, the Assyrian host is destroyed by the angel of the Lord, when eyes of the blind are opened, withered arms restored to energy, and bent backs straightened, and the dead raised out of the grave, then men know that God is at work. The miracle is the majestic seal which God has affixed to the revelation which He has given us. As Nicodemus said to Jesus, "No man can do the works which thou doest, except God be with him."

3. *Miracles are provable; they took place.* We have seen that miracles are antecedently possible and that they are antecedently probable. Now we shall see that they actually took place. "This beginning of miracles did Jesus in Cana of Galilee," says John after the account of turning the water into wine, "and manifested forth his glory." It was the "beginning" of miracles. In other words, Jesus from the commencement to the end of His public ministry wrought many miracles. Christianity claims to be a revelation from God confirmed and vindicated by mighty signs and wonders. The Gospels contain the records of thirty-three miracles and tell us that there were many others which they do not record. Try to take those stories out of the Four Gospels, and how much of a Christ have you left? The miracles are as a strand woven into the fabric of the garment of Christ's personality, and you cannot tear them out without destroying the fabric itself. The poor, minor, damaged Christ which some men try to hold up after they have banished the miraculous in the life of Jesus is not a Christ that the world has taken, or will take, seriously. The only Christ that we

know is the Christ who walked on the sea, raised the dead, and called the dead out of their graves. If these are not facts, then the fact of Christ is gone. But what is the evidence for the facts?

All that evidence is contained in the New Testament. There can be no doubt as to the meaning of the evidence or the nature of the events witnessed to. Hume, in his celebrated essay on the miracles, took the stand that miracles were so far beyond our ordinary experience that when we come upon an account of them we must take the view that falsehood and self-deception are always more probable than that the miracles actually took place. But when we come to the witness of the New Testament we are confronted by the difficulty of believing that the men who relate the miracles are either deceivers or deceived. No one can read these accounts without being impressed with the humility, sincerity, and deep piety of the men who tell them or write them. If they were conscienceless fabricators, how was it that such men produced that picture of moral excellence before whom all the ages have fallen down in reverent admiration? How could men who lied about the facts of Christ's life have produced so marvelous a character? Of this, at least, we may be sure, the men who relate the miracles of Jesus were not conscious deceivers and liars.

But could they have been mistaken? Was their eye filmed with enthusiasm when they wrote, so that they imagined events which never took place? Or when they saw these events, were they only natural happenings, which they in their love and zeal magnified into the miraculous? Was it an optical delusion which made the disciples think that Jesus was walking on the sea, when He was only walking on the shore near which the ship was tossing? Was the widow of Nain's son only apparently dead? But these men were not credulous, moonstruck fools; on the contrary, they were hard-headed, practical men whom Jesus in the resurrection had to rebuke for their unwillingness to believe that He had risen from the dead. Then, the miraculous events to which they bear witness were not the kind which men readily imagine to have taken place.

No one, by the most exalted imagination or enthusiastic ecstasy, would think that a man had fed a multitude of five thousand with five loaves and two small fishes. No one would imagine that a man, three days in the grave, had risen. Not only were the events of such a nature that they could not have been imagined to have taken place by some enthusiast, but they are of the kind which admit of easy verification. The enemies of Christ, for instance, resorted to every known expedient to overthrow the witness of the man born blind that Jesus had healed him. But he proved beyond all doubt that he was the man born blind, and that Jesus had opened his eyes. Tried by every test, the evidence for the miracles stands. Falsehood or deception in the records of the life of Jesus as written by men of such sincerity, and sobriety, and common sense, and honesty, would constitute a greater miracle than all the miracles put together.

But the chief witness to the miracles is Jesus Himself. We require no better witness than Matthew, and John, and Mark, and Luke, to convince us of the historicity of the miracles. But God in His grace has given us a far greater witness. That witness is Christ Himself. In his book, *My Belief*, Dr. Robert F. Horton, speaking of the miracles, says, "No wise apologist aware of the nature of evidence and of the evidence of Christianity, would identify the faith in Jesus with belief in the miracles recorded in the Gospels."

He goes on to say that in the future there will be many who will not accept the miracles of the Gospels, but will still believe in Christ. But we remember that Christ Himself in the most solemn way declared that He worked miracles. When John sent from the dungeon in his doubt and said to Jesus, "Art thou he that should come, or look we for another?" Jesus said to his messengers, "Go and tell John the things which ye see and hear: the blind receive their sight, the lame walk, the lepers are cleansed, and the deaf hear, and the dead are raised up, and the poor have the gospel preached unto them."

You tell me you do not believe that Jesus walked on the sea, or opened the eyes of the blind, or made the deaf hear, or the dumb speak; all that you rule out. But you say you do take the teachings of Jesus. But do you take this teaching? Do you accept Jesus when He Himself says that He made the blind see and raised the dead? On two different occasions Jesus referred to the miracle He had worked in feeding the multitude in the wilderness with the five loaves and the two small fishes. Just as the only Jesus we know is the Jesus who worked miracles, so the only Jesus we know is the Jesus who claimed that He worked miracles, testified in the most deliberate way that He did. But what sort of a man was this Jesus whom people, today, say they will take and worship, minus His miracles? They all agree that He was a perfect character.

But how was He a perfect character if He did not work miracles, yet testified that He did? The holiest character who has appeared on the horizon of human thought, the kindest, truest, best, the One from whose brow truth flashed as the rays of light pour from the orient sun, bears witness that He worked miracles and did many mighty wonders. Which shall we accept, the witness of men who devise clever hypotheses to do away with the supernatural in Christianity, or the witness of Christ?

The Meaning of the Miracles

1. *The miracles witnessed to Christ as the Son of God and thus served to authenticate the Christian revelation as from God.* In other words, the miracles tell us, as they were designed to tell us, that Christianity is true. It is a great thing for any man to claim that he fulfills all prophecy; it is a great thing for a man to claim the absolute love and allegiance of men; it is a great thing for a man to claim that his kingdom is an everlasting kingdom and that after heaven and earth shall have passed away his words shall still stand; it is a great thing for a man to say that he is God, and that by virtue of his sacrificial death men's sins shall be forgiven. The man who makes such claims must come into court with extraordinary evidence and witness. Christ is accompanied by such evidence—the miracles: "Jesus of Nazareth, a man approved of God unto you by miracles."

Nothing could be more certain than that the miracles attest the divine nature and the redemptive authority of Jesus. We have adverted to what He said to John. John the Baptist wanted to know if Jesus was He who should come, that is, the Messiah, the Lamb of God who takes away the sins of the world. Christ said that He was, and in proof of the claim, told John of the miracles He had worked. He said that because He was able to cast out devils the power of God had come upon men. By His miracles, says John, Christ manifested His glory. Nicodemus, on the ground of His miracles, concluded that Jesus was a teacher come from God. Peter says in the words of our text that Christ was approved a man of God among the people of Jerusalem by miracles and wonders and signs.

After Jesus had forgiven a man his sins and His audience were aghast and outraged at such a fearful claim on His part, Jesus then proceeded to make the paralyzed man walk, and said, as He did so, that it was a sign of His right and His power to forgive sin: "But that ye may know that the Son of man hath power on earth to forgive sin, I say unto thee, Rise, take up thy bed and walk!" It was the miracles that made the disciples believe in Jesus, and they, in turn, made the world believe in Christ.

2. *The miracles illustrate and explain the teaching of Jesus.* That which proves Christ also explains Him. More sermons are preached on the miracles of Jesus than on His parables, for the miracles help to explain the parables. Take out from the sacred narratives the miracles of Jesus, and the tender pathos, the sweet beauty of the Gospels is gone. It is one thing to hear Jesus talk; it is another to see Him in action. In the miracles, we see Christ dealing tenderly and yet majestically with our human lives and their sins and burdens and sorrows and fears. We see Him walk on the sea at the fourth hour of the night, and we know that in the storms of pain and grief, when all our life's sea is convulsed with a tempest, Christ is with us. We hear His voice as the storm-tossed disciples did, and immediately we know that love is near us and about us. We see Him cast out the demons, and we know that in proportion as we live with Him, the unclean spirits leave us. We see Him take pity on the paralytic, and we know that no life is so poor, weak, discounted by the world but Christ loves it. We see Him open the eyes of Bartimaus and we learn how faith, faith that clings to Christ and will not let Him go, shall have its own. We see Him stop the funeral procession on the road to the cemetery at Nain, and raise the widow's son, and we know that in our deepest and darkest sorrow, when the cloud hangs so thick about us that we know not which way to turn and our eyes through their tears can see no path, Jesus is present to sympathize with us and tell of His covenant love. We see Him raise Lazarus from the dead and say, "He that believeth in me shall never die, and though he were dead yet shall he live," and we are able to believe that the grave is not our end, and that in Christ we shall live forever.

5

WAS CHRIST THE SON OF GOD?

The Son of God, who loved me, and gave himself for me (Gal. 2:20).

All of Christianity, the length and the breadth and the depth and the height of the redeeming love of God, is gathered together in that one sentence of St. Paul, as the whole glory of the sun is mirrored in a drop of dew. "The Son of God who loved me and gave himself for me." The two great needs of our fallen and lost humanity are love and forgiveness. Man needs tenderness and pity, but he also needs cleansing from sin. The heart of mankind yearns for love, yet the world cannot give it what it desires. History, nature, what we call civilization, they know nothing of One who loves us and who gave Himself for us. There is nothing there to tell us that God is love, or that He has a Son who has died for us. All that we see there is a hell of passion, and strife, and cruelty, and tears, and blood. "Tears and blood drops have been innumerable, and the shores of eternity have been beaten on incessantly by the waves of sorrow and trouble that have rolled in from this world." But here is a man, and with him millions of others who have passed through the fires and wilderness of life, who says, "The life that I now live, I live in faith, the faith which is in the Son of God, who loved me and gave himself for me."

Our faith as Christians rests upon these three facts, that Jesus Christ is God's Son, that He loved us, that He died for us. If this be true, then all our needs are met. Sin, pain, sorrow, death, separation, agony, death, can never be the same. The whole universe of life is changed. In Browning's *Death in the Desert*, where he imagines the death and the last words of St. John, the Evangelist says,

> I say, the acknowledgment of God in Christ,
> Accepted by thy reason, solves for thee
> All questions in the earth and out of it.

Yes, if God was in Christ, and if He loved me and gave Himself for me, then all problems are solved and all wants are satisfied.

> Thou, O Christ, art all I need.
> More than all in Thee I find.

But if Christ was not the Son of God, who died for us, then chaos is come again.

> The pillar'd firmament is rottenness,
> And earth's firm base is built on stubble.

As I have reviewed once more the evidence in the Scriptures which proves to us that Jesus was the Son of God and that God was in Christ reconciling the world to Himself, the thought has come again into my mind, How could any person who pretended to get his knowledge of Jesus from the Bible—the only place where we have any information about Him—think that Jesus was only a man? Still more, how could any church have arisen which took as its foundation the non-deity of Jesus Christ? What will they do with the New Testament? By what strange process is it that they rule out the Son of Sod and leave us only Jesus of Nazareth? The only way I know of, is the way Thomas Jefferson did it; he just took his pen and ran it through the passages which spake of Christ as God, through the miracles done upon Him or done through Him, through any passage which shows Him more than man. His Gospel thus came to a close with the words, "And they rolled a great stone to the door of the sepulchre and departed." That is the end of Jesus! And if that is all, then you have rolled a great stone to the door of the world's one and only hope. And upon what ground? Upon no ground whatever, for the only Christ is the Christ of the New Testament, and that Christ was the Son of God.

In reviewing the evidence for this, one is embarrassed by the wealth of the material. The only difficulty is to make a selection. In this chapter I shall deal for the greater part with the testimony of Christ Himself, and then briefly with the corroboration of that testimony by Christian experience.

THE TESTIMONY OF CHRIST

1. *Indirect testimony*. By this I mean that without directly saying that He was God, or the Son of God, Jesus made claim to distinctions and powers which could be predicated of no man. He claimed pre-existence, saying, "Before Abraham was, I am"; "I came down from heaven"; "Glorify thou me with the glory which I had with thee before the world was" (John 8:58; 6:38; 17:5). He claimed omnipotence, for He said, "All power is given unto me in heaven and on earth." He claimed infallibility: "Heaven and earth shall pass away, but my words shall never pass away." And not only infallibility, but He claimed to be truth itself: "I am the way, the truth, and the life." He claimed to be sinless, and challenged His foes to convict Him of any sin. In His whole ministry and teaching, though He comes to seek and to save sinners, He always takes the position of one who is separate from sinners. He claimed an exclusive dominion over the souls of men, calling upon men to leave all and follow Him and declaring that even the closest of domestic ties must not stand in the way of allegiance to Him. When He is about to die He gives His friends a Supper, a sacrament which they are to celebrate solely in memory of Him, "This do in remembrance of me." He claimed an exclusive and peculiar knowledge of God, saying, "No man knoweth the Father but the Son." He speaks to the disciples about "your Father," and teaches them to pray beginning, "Our Father," but He also speaks of "My" Father, and never identifies His relationship to the Father with that of the disciples.

He claimed omnipresence, telling the disciples that He would be with them to the end of the world. He claimed the right to forgive sin, and the indignant and shocked scribes and Pharisees, if they did not regard Him as the Son of God, were correct when they protested, "Who but God can forgive sin?" He said to His disciples He would give them what the world could not give them:

"My peace I give unto you. Not as the world giveth, give I unto you." From the beginning of His ministry to the very end He claimed to be Messiah, that is, the Christ, the one predicted in the Old Testament. But the Messiah was regarded as the Son of God. This is shown by the high priest's question to Jesus at His trial, "Tell us, Art thou the Christ, the Son of God?"

More than seventy times in the Gospels Jesus applies to Himself the title, Son of Man. What did He mean by that? If He was just a man, there would be no sense in announcing Himself as such, any more than there would be sense in your emphasizing what everybody sees and knows, that every man is a son of man. But Jesus called Himself "The" Son of Man. It is a title taken from the Book of Daniel, where it was foretold that the powers of this earth should crumble before the Ancient of Days and one like unto the Son of Man, coming with the clouds of heaven, whose kingdom and dominion should be universal and everlasting. That is what Jesus means when He refers to Himself as the Son of Man. No ordinary son of man, "a" son of man, answers to the implication of the title, but only "The" Son of Man, who was also the Son of God, or our Redeemer, the God-Man, Jesus Christ.

Jesus claimed the right finally to examine and judge and sentence men. He makes the stupendous claim that before Him shall be gathered all the nations of the earth, and that men are to be accepted or rejected and punished with everlasting doom upon the ground of their attitude towards Him. "Inasmuch as ye have done it unto one of the least of these, ye have done it unto me." These extraordinary claims—pre-existence, infallibility, sinlessness, absolute dominion over men's souls, exclusive knowledge of God, omnipresence, the right to forgive sin and mediate between God and man, that He was the Messiah, the Son of Man, the Judge of the quick and the dead, He sealed by His death. In the agony and trial which accompanied His death there was never the least suggestion of withdrawing a single one of His great claims, or acknowledging that He was either mistaken or wicked. On the contrary, He reiterated them in the most solemn and final manner. Whether or not there was any such man as Jesus, this we know—that the Jesus whose life is related in the New Testament claimed rank and power which belong to no man, and which can belong only to God.

2. *Direct Testimony.* Not only did Jesus lay claim to divine power and rank, but He repeatedly and definitely said that He was God, or the Son of God. Perhaps the most impressive and striking example of this occurred when Jesus met with His disciples at Caesarea Philippi and said to them carefully and deliberately, "Who do men say that I, the Son of Man, am?" The time had now come for a plain statement on the subject of His person and rank. Some of the people thought that He was Elijah, others, John the Baptist, risen from the dead, others, Jeremiah, or one of the great prophets —they were not sure which. But Jesus pressed the question closer, "Who say ye that I am?" Then from the lips of Peter came the great answer, "Thou art the Christ, the Son of the living God."

This confession of Peter Jesus accepted unreservedly and with exceeding joy, exclaiming, "Blessed art thou, Simon, Bar-jona; for flesh and blood hath not revealed it unto thee, but my Father which is in heaven. And I say also unto thee, That thou art Peter, and upon this rock I will build my church; and the gates of hell shall not prevail against it." Whether we take the Catholic view of a primacy given to Peter here as the rock, or the common Protestant view that by the rock Christ meant the confession Peter made, all must agree that Jesus in this most solemn way shows to His disciples that the great and the grand thing about Him is the fact that He is the Son of God. What He declared here, as prophecy, has been fulfilled. The Church was founded upon the rock of the Divine Sonship of Jesus, and that is the only reason why the gates of hell have not prevailed, and shall not prevail, against it.

After Jesus had healed the man born blind, and the scribes and Pharisees had cast him out because he insisted that Jesus had healed him, Jesus in His tender compassion found the poor outcast and said to him, "Dost thou believe on the Son of God?" He answered and said, "Who is he, Lord, that I may believe on him?" Jesus said unto him, "Thou hast both seen him, and he it is that speaketh with thee." And he said, Lord, I believe. "And he worshipped him."

That Jesus clearly and repeatedly claimed to be God is evident from the attitude of His enemies. Back of all His human foes was the arch-foe of every soul, the devil himself. In the Temptation, the account of which could have come from Jesus only, the devil said to Jesus, "If thou be the Son of God, command that these stones be made bread." That was equivalent to saying, "You claim to be the Son of God; if you are, then prove it by this miracle." When the Jews, angry at His incisive teaching and preaching, took up stones to stone Him, Jesus asked them for which of His good works they were going to stone Him? They replied, "For a good work we stone thee not, but because that thou, being a man, makest thyself God." That was their chief rage at Him, that He claimed to be the Son of God. At His trial when the perjured witnesses could not fabricate sufficient evidence upon which to condemn Jesus before the council of the Jews, the high priest swept the whole mass of false testimony aside by coming directly to the point and asking Jesus to say whether or not He was the Son of God. "I adjure thee by the living God, that thou tell us whether thou art the Christ, the Son of God. Jesus saith unto him, Thou hast said."

How anyone can go through the Gospels and not be confronted everywhere by the deity of Christ, either implied in the mighty claims He makes, or directly asserted by Christ, is a mystery. Yet there are still those who pretend to do it. As I have already said, the only way in which they do it is the way Thomas Jefferson did it, namely, to go through the Gospels and deliberately cut out all those passages which refer to His divine power and nature. When you have done that, you have taken away Christ Himself. You have not even a few fragments which you can piece into a harmonious whole.

The character of Jesus is humanity's one great moral asset. Truth and sincerity shone in His face as the stars in the face of the night. Directly and indirectly, by teaching and by miracle, by direct asseveration and by accepting the witness, or the worship, or the taunting, of others, Jesus bore witness that He was the Son of God. If He is not, then He was a bad man. *Aut deus aut non bonus homo*. There is no other alternative. A preacher in New York said, not so long ago—he is one of those who think to save some sort of a Jesus out of the wreck of Christ's divinity—"What is God? We call God the power which is responsible for the universe—its creation and continuation. But we may as well face facts. Christ was a wonderful man, a beautiful character. He was the superlative of anything you may choose to call Him. But to say that a man born upon this earth, created by the power of God, had the power of this God of creation is superstition. We may accept the spiritual teachings of Christ as the basis of our religion, but we need not believe that He ascended and is seated upon the right hand of God."

There could be nothing so impossible or absurd as such a Christ. If Christ was not the Son of God as He claimed to be, as all His disciples took Him to he, and for claiming to be which all His enemies hated Him and killed Him, then, instead of being the beautiful teacher, the superlative of almost anything you choose to call Him, Jesus is either the superlative fool or the superlative knave and impostor of history. But we know that He was not a fool, for the man who utters these great teachings had intellect such as the world had never seen. And we know that He was not a liar or a knave, for such a man could never have won and held the devotion and the love of countless millions of beings.

The Testimony Outside of Christ: The Four Great Miracles

The first of these was the miracle of the Virgin Birth. In recent days we have heard men speak lightly of the Virgin Birth, as if it were a thing hard to accept and of no use when you did accept it. We wonder if people who talk thus have ever read the Bible at all. The angel who, according to the great historian, Luke, made the announcement to Mary, evidently thought differently of the Virgin Birth, for he said, "The Holy Spirit shall come upon thee and the power of the Most High shall overshadow thee; therefore also that holy thing which shall be born of thee shall be called the Son of God." The Virgin Birth to Mary, and in the course of time, when she made it known, to others also, bore witness to the Divine Sonship of her child.

Then there are the two miracles of utterance. First, the Voice at the baptism of Jesus when the Holy Spirit descended like a dove and a voice was heard saying, "This is my beloved Son, in whom I am well pleased. Hear ye him." The same sentence was spoken when He was on the Mount of Transfiguration.

But the one great miracle which proved the claim of Christ to be the Son of God, and that to which the apostles appealed in their preaching, was *the miracle of the Resurrection*. St. Paul, in the beginning of his letter to the Romans, speaks of Jesus Christ as one who was "declared to be the Son of God with power by the resurrection from the dead." They preached Christ everywhere as the Son of God who was the world's Redeemer, and the proof to which they appealed was His resurrection from the dead. Not only was it a mighty sign and wonder, but the very one that the prophets had foretold would show the power of God, to wit, that God would not suffer His Holy One to see corruption, but would raise Him from the dead.

Time would fail to tell of the rich testimony of the disciples and the apostles, how they worshipped Him as the Son of God, how they prayed to Him, how they built all their hopes on the fact that He was God, how they endured persecution and death rather than deny Him, and when they died, like Stephen, saw Him sitting at the right hand of God; and how all their future was painted with the glowing expectation of the day when He should come again, and they would be with Him forever. Just what people think they have left that is worth talking about when they have stripped Jesus of His divinity, it is difficult to see. Certainly not one who answers the two great needs of the human soul, the need for love, infinite love, and the need of forgiveness. The parlor philosopher may be interested in this Jesus who is the creation of fancy, but there is nothing about Him that will help or save the soul of a sinner. One hears quoted very often, and very thoughtlessly, Richard Watson Gilder's lines:

> If Jesus Christ be man
> (And only man), I say
> That of all mankind I will cleave to Him,
> And to Him will I cleave alway.
> If Jesus Christ be God
> (And the only God), I swear
> I will follow Him through heaven and hell,
> The earth, the sea, and the air.

The last part is sense and reason; the first part is nonsense. If Jesus Christ be man, and only a man, there is nothing in Him worth following and worth cleaving to. The poet sings as if it made little difference which way the vote fell, man, or Son of God. But it *does* make a difference, an awful, immeasurable difference. If Christ were not God, then we do not know that God is Love. If Christ be not God, we have no Savior who gave Himself as a ransom for our sins. If Christ be not God, we have no forgiveness. If Christ be not God, then death, and if not death, then hell, ends all. Those whom we have loved and lost awhile in this life we shall never, never behold again. Never! The world is just as dark as that pagan world into which Christ came when hope was dead. But if Christ be God, then we have a Rock, a Rock that is "higher than I"; a Rock against which all the storms of time and eternity shall sweep and break in vain.

> Rock of Ages, cleft for me,
> Let me hide myself in Thee!

6

DID CHRIST DIE FOR OUR SINS?

Christ died for our sins, according to the Scriptures (1 Cor. 15:3).

"I don't believe a word of it!

"You don't believe in the Atonement?" "No; I do not!"

"How, then, do you think that we are saved?"

"Saved? It depends upon what you mean by being saved."

"I mean just what the Bible does, when it speaks of being saved and being lost."

"I think we are saved by obeying the teachings of Jesus, by following His example and doing His will; not by His death."

The above colloquy took place at the close of a service in a Presbyterian Church where the minister had preached a sermon on the Atonement, or how Christ died for our sins. Standing by itself, such a comment, sad enough so far as the individual uttering it is concerned, would mean but little. But this man is the representative of a very large group. His sentiments can be heard, I suppose, in almost any Protestant Church. We might as well face the fact that two kinds of Christianity are being preached and taught in our Protestant churches today. One is a Christianity of ideals and inspiration and good works. Christ is preached as the great teacher, example, inspirer and leader. With some He is divine, with others He is only man, though the noblest flower which has bloomed on the stock of our humanity. This is a Christianity of instruction and education. If its disciples use the word "salvation," that is all that they mean.

The other kind of Christianity is the Christianity of redemption. Man is a sinner and under the condemnation of God's law. He could do nothing to save himself. But God sent His Only Begotten Son, Jesus Christ, to die for man, in place of man, as a substitute for man. By faith in Christ as Redeemer, man is forgiven, the guilt and the stain of his sin is taken away, and he is restored to the family of God. In the former kind of Christianity, the Christianity of education and ideals and inspiration, the death of Christ is but an incident, though a moving and beautiful incident. In the Christianity of redemption the death of Christ is the one grand truth around which gather all the other truths of the Christian religion. It is a fact eternal in its significance and universal in its application.

In the Christianity of redemption this truth takes the place in preaching which it did in the preaching of St. Paul, when he said to the Corinthians, "For I delivered unto you, *first of all*, how that Christ died for our sins, according to the Scriptures." If you take away the death of Christ from the man whose Christianity is the Christianity of education he is not much troubled, for he has the parables and the sayings of Jesus left. His religion is not impaired. But if you take away the death of Christ from the man whose Christianity is the Christianity of redemption, you have taken all that he has. His only hope is Christ crucified. On the crucifix where the death of our Lord on the Cross is portrayed you have read the Latin words, *Spes Unica*, the Only Hope. The man who feels that he is a sinner and must have a Savior greater than himself has no other hope but Christ crucified for his sins.

Regardless of denominational names and divisions, the real cleavage in Protestant Christianity today is along this line just indicated. There are really just two parties, those who think of Christianity as a religion of education and of inspiration and those who think of it as a religion of redemption for sinners; those who follow Christ as a leader, teacher, example, and those who trust in Him as a Redeemer. It will now be my purpose to show that the only true Christianity is the Christianity of Redemption and that the only real, historic Christ is the Christ who died for our sins on Calvary's Cross.

THAT CHRIST DIED FOR OUR SINS IS THE CHRISTIANITY OF THE APOSTLES

Before He died and after His resurrection, our Lord made provision for the preaching of His Gospel to all the world. The Gospels do not tell us how or what the apostles preached. But in the Acts of the Apostles and in the rest of the New Testament we have the plain and unmistakable record and account of what it was the Apostles preached, and therefore upon what kind of a foundation they built the Christian Church. I need not spend much time on this, for the fact is quickly and easily established by anyone who reads the pages of the Acts, or the Epistles, or the Book of Revelation.

1. *The testimony of St. Peter.* The great figure of the early Church was Peter. The weakest and most unworthy when Christ was delivered into the hands of His enemies and put to death on the Cross, Peter, forgiven and restored by Jesus after His resurrection, became the great leader and the great voice of the Church. The first pages of the book of the Acts preserve for us the outlines of Peter's effective and Pentecostal preaching. In substance it was this: Jesus of Nazareth, whom the Jews had crucified, was the Christ, the Son of God, the Messiah of whom the prophets had spoken, appointed to be the Judge and the Savior of men. Therefore it was the duty of men everywhere to repent of their sins and believe in Christ.

When they did this they would receive the remission of sins. That Jesus was the Christ, the Son of God, that He had been put to death, and that now men could have forgiveness of sin through faith in Him, that is the message Peter delivers whenever we hear him speak. In these first sermons he does not, directly, say that it is on the ground of the death of Jesus that men's sins are forgiven. But he does declare the great fact of remission of sins through Christ, that the great office of Christ is to forgive, and as proof that the men to whom he was speaking needed forgiveness of sin he cites the fact of the crime and sin of putting the Lord of Glory to death on the Cross.

Because Peter does not, in these first sermons, definitely tell men that the ground of their forgiveness is the death of Christ, some have thought that Peter, only seven weeks after the death of Christ, knew nothing of the doctrine of the atonement, or forgiveness of sin on the ground of the death of Christ. But Peter was speaking to Jews whose whole religious training and tradition taught them, through their sacrificial system, that without the shedding of blood there is no remission of sin. But if there is any doubt as to what Peter took to be the ground of forgiveness through Christ, that doubt is dispelled by his first epistle. In that great document Peter is writing to comfort and strengthen believers in Jesus Christ who are suffering persecution. He reminds them of their great hope, the inheritance, incorruptible and undefiled, and that fadeth not away, reserved for them in heaven. But what is it that he says to them in order to encourage them and make them persevere to the end?

Peter had been the companion of Jesus for three years. He had had an unusually intimate and dramatic relationship with Him. He must have remembered many of the comforting sayings of Christ, many of the merciful acts of Christ which would have been applicable to the case of these persecuted Christians. One might think Peter would have referred to some of those sayings and some of those acts. But there is not a word of this. The one great fact which he holds up before these troubled believers is the fact that Christ died for their sins. He exhorts them to fidelity by reminding them that they had been redeemed, not as slaves might be redeemed—and some of them no doubt were slaves—by silver and gold, but with Precious Blood, even the Blood of Christ. If some of them are suffering wrongfully, for offenses they have not committed, let them be comforted by remembering that Jesus, who was sinless, also suffered, dying on the Cross not for His own sins, but for our sins—"who His own self bare our sins in His body on the tree, that we having died unto sin might live unto righteousness."

And not only Peter, but all the other apostles who speak in the New Testament, when they are urging men to their duty in this life and pressing upon them the Christian virtues, never appeal to the sayings of our Lord, which might have been aptly quoted, but almost invariably derive their motives for the discharge of Christian duty and their confirmation of Christian hope from the death and passion of Christ, from those hours of shame and anguish in which our Lord's earthly ministry closed. Why were they so silent about what preachers today are so vocal, the courage, sanctity, wisdom, compassion of Jesus? It was because that although they had been with Jesus, the great fact they now saw as they looked back and looked forward, was the fact of His death for the sins of the world, that He died for our sins.

2. *St. John.* We pass by his teaching in the Fourth Gospel, for that belongs more to the testimony of Jesus. In his first letter John makes it plain that he believes man is a sinner and in need of a Savior. He says that the whole world lies in sin, and that whoever says he has no sin is a liar and the truth is not in him. He also teaches that God forgives the man who confesses his sin. To this he adds the definite Christian message of the relationship of Jesus and His death to the forgiveness of sin, telling us that the blood of Jesus, His Son, cleanses us from all sin, and God's love is explained and demonstrated and proffered to man by the death of Christ: "Herein is love, not that we loved God, but that He loved us and sent His Son to be the propitiation for our sins." In the Apocalypse, amid so much that is obscure and phantasmal, the one clear, predominant, sublime and unmistakable figure is that of the Lamb who was slain for the sins of men. From the wrath of the Lamb, whose mercy they have scorned, the wicked implore the mountains and the rocks to fall on them and hide them, and to the Lamb the redeemed saints, they who have come up out of great tribulation and washed their robes and made them white in the blood of the Lamb, sing all their resounding psalms of praise and honor.

3. *The Letter to the Hebrews.* The authorship of this epistle is disputed, but no one disputes the meaning of it, for its one idea, illustrated and explained in so many ways, is that Christ is mankind's great High Priest who, through the Eternal Spirit, offered Himself as sacrifice unto God for our sins, making a sacrifice which, unlike that of Israel's high priest on the day of atonement, can never be repeated, for it was done once for all.

4. *St. Paul.* It is unnecessary to state what Paul taught about the death of Christ. A striking proof of the place he gave to the death of Christ as a death atoning for our sins is found in the fact that just at present the chief effort of those who reject Christianity as a

religion of redemption from sins by the death of Christ is to discredit this idea of Christianity by saying that it is an idea that comes from St. Paul, but does not come from Jesus. Wherever one opens the writings of St. Paul it is the Cross of which he is speaking. Wherever he goes he is determined to know among the people nothing save Jesus Christ and Him crucified. He delivered unto men first of all, that Christ died for our sins according to the Scriptures. He would not glory, save in the Cross. The great evidence of the love of God for man was just the same with Paul as it was with John—"God commendeth his love towards us in that while we were yet sinners, Christ died for us." Had we opened that great heart, which Chrysostom called the heart of the world, we would have found upon it these words, "The Son of God, who loved me and gave himself for me."

In this brief sketch we have seen what place the death of Christ for our sins took in the preaching of the men who established the Church in the world. When, therefore, we listen to men, or read men, who today know better than Peter and Paul and John did, the meaning of Christianity, and who tell us that it has some other meaning than this, that Christ died for our sins, let us remember that however clever and learned these men are, and however much followed after by the multitude, who say as the multitude said of Herod when he made the people an oration, "It is the voice of a god, and not of a man!"—let us remember that this preaching of Christianity was not the preaching which established the Church in the world and established it so firmly that the storms of the centuries have not overthrown it. The preaching which established Christianity in the world was the preaching of the Cross, the forgiveness of sin through the death of Christ.

The Testimony of Jesus

We have seen what the answer of the apostles is to our question, Did Christ die for our sins? What is the answer of Jesus Himself? Is His answer the same as that of the apostles? the same as that of Peter and Paul and John? Everything depends upon this.

1. *The pre-eminent place given in the Gospels to the story* of the death of Christ would suggest to us that their authors would not

have given so much space to the death of Jesus unless there had been something in the words of Jesus and the attitude of Jesus which made them feel that His death was the one great fact in comparison with which all else was subsidiary. Such events as the birth of Jesus, His temptation, His Transfiguration, the Lord's Supper, and even the Ascension into Heaven, are missing from one or more of the Gospels. But all of the Gospels relate with the fullest detail, the death of Christ.

2. *The sayings of Jesus about His death are the natural explanation* of this united and elaborated testimony about it in the Four Gospels. In other words, after what Jesus said about His death it was natural for men who wrote the story of His life to give preeminence to the fact of His death. At the first passover He said, "Destroy this temple and in three days I will raise it up"—meaning the temple of His body. To Nicodemus, a few days afterward, He said that "As Moses lifted up the serpent in the wilderness, even so must the Son of Man be lifted up." When the Jews insisted upon a sign, He said that as Jonah was in the belly of the whale, even so the Son of Man should be three days and three nights in the heart of the earth. In His parable of the Good Shepherd, He referred to His approaching death, and again in His parable of how the husbandmen killed the heir and son. Most tenderly, too, when the disciples rebuked Mary for the costly gift of the ointment and pure spikenard which she had poured over His head and His feet, He counseled them to let her alone, for she had kept it against the day of His burying. When the Greeks came to visit Him, in His moods of alternate jubilation and dread He cried out, "I, if I be lifted up, will draw all men unto me." On the Mount of Transfiguration He spoke with Moses and Elijah concerning His decease which He should accomplish at Jerusalem.

Nor were His references to His death just occasional or incidental, for at least three of the evangelists tell us that in the most direct and careful and positive way He taught the disciples both the fact and the manner of His death—that He would be betrayed into the hands of the Jewish rulers, who in turn would hand Him over to the Gentiles, that is, the Romans, who would put Him to death by crucifixion. For the beginning of this instruction Jesus chose one of the most impressive moments of His ministry, when

Peter had publicly confessed Him as the Son of the living God. "From that time forth began Jesus to shew unto his disciples how that he must go to Jerusalem and suffer many things of the elders and chief priests and scribes, and be killed, and be raised again the third day" (Matt. 16:21). "Let these sayings sink down into your ears: for the Son of man shall be delivered into the hands of men" (Luke 9:44).

3. *The attitude of Jesus towards His death*, or what He felt about it rather than what He said about it. I shall cite three instances of the depth and peculiarity of the feeling of Jesus towards His death.

a. Towards Peter. When Peter had confessed Him as the Messiah, the Son of God, and Jesus had told the disciples of His rejection and crucifixion, Peter, thinking that such a fate was impossible for the Son of God, cried out, "Be it far from thee, Lord: this shall not be unto thee." But Jesus said, "Get thee behind me, Satan: for thou art an offence unto me; for thou savorest not the things that be of God, but those that be of men." The only explanation of the terrible rebuke given to the man whom, but a moment before, Jesus had publicly thanked and praised for his confession, is that Christ's future crucifixion and death was a terrible reality to Him, that He recognizes in it the climax of His ministry of reconciliation, and that he who tempts Him to turn back from it, is His enemy and the enemy of mankind.

b. Towards the Greeks. When He first heard of the visit of the Greeks and their wish to see Him, Jesus rejoiced in spirit, as He saw the future conquests of the Cross, and said, "The hour is come that the Son of Man should be glorified." But when He thought of the price that He was to pay, of the rejection, the shame and the death, He cried out, "Father, save me from this hour!" In this hour which was to mark His glory, the hour of His death, there was also that which was terrible and overwhelming.

c. Gethsemane. Why did Christ not meet His death calmly and without evidence of distress and anguish, as Socrates, or many another noble man has met cruel, painful, and unmerited death? There is but one answer, but one explanation of that strange scene in the Garden of Gethsemane, the pathetic but vain appeal to the sleeping disciples, the intense agony which brought the blood from His brow, the imploring cry, "O, my Father, if it be possible, let this cup pass from me," and this is that it is not physical death with its cruel and dark accompaniments that Jesus is shrinking from, but a death such as no man before had ever died, and that is, a death from sin. The strange agony was that of a man whose soul was to be made an offering for a sin, and that man, One who knew no sin, One who was the Beloved Son of God.

4. *The Sign that He gave the Church.* He taught them by His words and He taught them by His strange and awful attitude towards His death that His death had a preeminent place in His Gospel, that it was death for sin, bearing for us the guilt and the punishment of sin. But lest there should be any misapprehension or unreadiness to believe, Jesus taught His disciples—and all who through them have come to believe in Him—by a sign, the beautiful sign of the Lord's Supper.

This Supper was to be observed unto the end of the world, until He should come again. When He broke the bread, He said, "This is my body which is broken for you." When He gave them the cup, He said, "Drink ye all of it, for this is my blood of the new covenant which is shed for many for the remission of sins." We have three accounts of the institution of the Supper in the Gospels and one in the writings of Paul. Each of them differs from the other as to the precise words used by Jesus, but all agree in the preservation of the same fundamental idea, that His death was for others, and for others who were sinners. Christ worked great miracles; yet He never said, "This miracle is done for the remission of sins." He preached great sermons, yet He never said at the end of a sermon, "This sermon is preached for the remission of sins." He was transfigured on the Mount, but not for the remission of sins; He was tempted of the devil, but He did not say it was for the remission of sins. But He did say that His death was for the remission of sins.

Such, then, is the answer to our question, "Did Christ die for our sins?" The Lord Jesus, by His words and by His sobs and tears, and by the Sacrament which He gave to His Church, and by His teaching to His disciples after His resurrection, said that His death was for our sins. The apostles, whom He sent forth to preach His Gospel in all the world, declared that Christ died for our sins, and upon that truth they built the Church.

Christianity knows nothing but the Cross. Without the Cross, without the death of Christ for our sins, there is no Christianity. Take out the Cross, and the music of Christianity dies into terrible silence, and the glory of it fades into darkness. The Son of God crucified for our sins is our only hope. In His name I lift Him up, this Christ who is still able to save the prodigal and wastrel, the beggar and millionaire, the illiterate and philosopher, the indifferent and the scoffer. We do not need to wait to believe until we can understand how it is that the death of the just man is the ground of the forgiveness of the unjust man. Paul did not know, and John did not know, and Peter did not know. Yet that was what they believed, and that was what they preached. All that we are asked to do is to believe. "And as Moses lifted up the serpent in the wilderness, even so must the Son of Man be lifted up: that whosoever believeth in him should not perish, but have eternal life."

7

DID CHRIST RISE FROM THE DEAD?

They entered in and found not the body of the Lord Jesus (Luke 24:3).

No one ever found it! The grave of Jesus is still without a tenant. "For the historian," writes Renan, "the life of Jesus finishes with His last sigh." But the life of the Christian commences with the Resurrection. The empty tomb was the cradle of the Church. If those women who came early to the tomb, or the disciples who came after them, had been able to find the body of Jesus, there or elsewhere, there never would have been a Christian Church.

The Resurrection of Jesus is a fact of spiritual significance. Nevertheless, it is a fact, and as such, must come into court and be examined and tested by the laws of evidence. In answering the question, "Did Christ rise from the dead?" our task will be to set forth the evidence for the fact of the Resurrection of Jesus from the dead. In doing this we shall first show that the belief in the Resurrection of Christ created the Christian Church; and secondly, we shall show the ground upon which that belief rested.

BELIEF IN THE RESURRECTION CREATED THE CHRISTIAN CHURCH

It is impossible for us to look upon any given effect without knowing in our inmost soul that there must have been a corresponding and sufficient cause. No one doubts that the Christian Church is here in the world, and has been here for centuries. Wherever you go in the world today, you will find Christian people holding Christian views and worshipping Jesus Christ. It would be impossible to write a history of the world for the past nineteen centuries and not in every page find it necessary to say something about the Christian Church, and the influence it has exerted on the affairs of mankind, the way it has guided the people's thought and hope, the physical and intellectual controversies which have been waged over the interpretation of its doctrines, even the cruel and wicked things that have often been done in its name. Wherever you turn, this great fact confronts you—Christianity.

The question then is, How did the Church come to be? Whence did it come? What cause produced this effect? The answer of Christianity itself is very clear and direct: The Church was established in the earth by the Resurrection of Jesus from the dead. No one would say that the birth of Jesus created the Church. Jesus might have performed all the miracles which are attributed to Him in the Gospels, have spoken all the parables and preached all the sermons that are recorded there, and at the end of His life been crucified and buried. But without the fact of the Resurrection you have no sufficient cause which explains Christianity. In spite of all that Jesus had said about His death being a death for the sin of the world, His death, alone, would not have created faith in Him, or established a Christian Church.

An onlooker like the Roman centurion in charge of the crucifixion might have been momentarily impressed with the way the man died, and the supernatural signs, such as the great darkness; but still we have nothing which accounts for the Christian Church. This is the more apparent when we discover in the Gospels that the death and burial of Jesus practically destroyed all faith in Him as the Messiah and the Son of God. It did not destroy affection for Him; but it is plain that only that loving reminiscence was left. The women came to anoint His body and are distressed to find the body removed from the grave. The disciples had hoped that this was the deliverer of Israel, the Messiah of God, as He had often told them He was. But nothing is plainer than that that hope had perished. It is impossible to conceive of the establishment of Christianity and the beginning of the Church without a belief in the Resurrection.

This is recognized even by those who deny Christianity and the great miracle which accounts for it, for they tell us that although Christ did not rise from the dead, it was the belief in the resurrection which explains the establishment of the Church. The whole question then hinges upon the subject of the origin of the belief: How did the belief arise? Did a great external fact create the belief, or did the belief spring from a delusion, some sort of a misunderstanding? Christianity says the belief arose through the Fact of the Resurrection. Christ has been crucified. The last pang has been felt, the last insult received and the final and awful penalty of sin tasted, the withdrawal of God's presence, causing the cry, "My God, my God, why hast thou forsaken me?" Nicodemus and Joseph of Arimathea take the body down from the Cross, embalm it according to the Jewish custom, and then lay it away in the new and rockhewn tomb in the garden, where they roll a great stone to the door of the sepulchre and depart. Friday night passes, and the Sabbath. Early on the first day of the week a few women come through the lifting mists to the sepulchre, not to see a risen Lord, but to weep at His tomb and anoint His dead body. It was a farewell to hope. That was at the beginning of the day. But before the day came to an end there was in, and about Jerusalem, a company of men and women holding the belief that was to turn the world upside down and turn the stream of history into a new channel. It was the belief that Christ was risen.

Because they believed that they had seen Him, the depressed and discouraged men who had been His disciples were suddenly changed into men of tremendous enthusiasm who go forth to face a world undauntedly and preach "Jesus and the Resurrection." Today, that same message is preached in the pulpits of the Old and New World. It is sung to the gorgeous ritual of the Greek Catholic Church in Athens, Moscow and Petrograd, and underneath the mighty dome of St. Peter's at Rome. The Scottish peasants hear it in their kirks in the Highlands of Scotland, while the sturdy mountaineers of the Waldensian valleys listen to the same message.

In the bleak solitudes of the Arctic regions the story of Jesus is told, and the natives of the South Seas chant it to the accompaniment of ocean waves breaking upon coral shores. In darkest Africa, and in highest Tibet, some one has told the story of Jesus and His power to save. The whole earth has been girdled with the melody of Christian psalms and hymns, as the disciples of Jesus on the first day of the week, the day upon which they believe their Lord rose from the dead, gather to honor His name and reconsecrate themselves to His service. The belief in the Resurrection created the Church, established it in the world, and has kept it in the world for more than nineteen centuries.

THE EVIDENCE FOR THE RESURRECTION

What, then, is the evidence for the Resurrection as a fact? No one doubts the fact that the belief created the Church. But does the belief itself rest upon fact? *A priori*, that so beneficent an institution as the Christian Church, teaching such pure morality and holding before humanity such grand hopes, has been created by belief in the Resurrection is an indirect witness to the credibility of the fact of the Resurrection, for it is difficult to understand how a huge delusion could have established Christianity in the world and kept it in the world through all these centuries. But we proceed to the direct witness to the fact of the Resurrection.

1. *The Predictions of Jesus Himself.* He explicitly and repeatedly foretold His Resurrection. When the scribes and Pharisees asked for a sign of His right to make the extraordinary claims He was making for Himself, Jesus said that as Jonah was three days and three nights in the belly of the whale, so the Son of man should be three days and three nights in the heart of the earth. He told the disciples that He was to be delivered into the hands of the Gentiles to be mocked, and scourged, and crucified, and that on the third day He would rise again. These predictions were known, not only to the friends of Jesus, who did not seem to take them seriously, but also to the enemies of Jesus who paid much more attention to them, for when Jesus had been crucified and buried, the scribes and Pharisees asked Pilate for a special guard at the tomb, saying, "Sir, we remember that that deceiver said, while He was yet alive, After three days I will rise again."

But, someone may say, because Jesus predicted that He would

rise again from the dead is no proof that He did rise, for that is a witness before the event and not after it. That is true. But the argument is good to this extent, that it proves that the Resurrection was in keeping with the character and claims of Jesus, for if, after saying so many times that He would rise from the dead, He did not rise, then, either Jesus was one of the biggest fools or the greatest knaves of all history. He was either pitifully ignorant and self-deceived, or a great deceiver and impostor—"that deceiver," as the Pharisees called Him. But the intellectual strength and the moral beauty of the character of Jesus, granted by men of all schools of thought, make it impossible to think of Him as either a fool or a deceiver. I state this by way of preparation so that when the evidence of the witness of the Resurrection is presented, we shall see how it agrees with what Jesus had said.

2. *The Witness of St. Paul.* So far as the records go, the earliest and most carefully arranged testimony to the Resurrection of Jesus is found in the fifteenth chapter of Paul's first letter to the Corinthians. He was nearer to the time of the death of Jesus than we are today to the battle of Manila Bay. In this passage Paul sums up the Christian message how Christ died for our sins according to the Scriptures, and was raised up the third day, according to the Scriptures. He cites six different appearances of Jesus after His Resurrection: to Peter, to the Twelve, to five hundred at one time, to James, to all the apostles, and last of all to himself, as one "born out of due time." The special appearance which made Paul believe in the Resurrection of Jesus was the stupendous transaction on the road to Damascus. Yet, when he sums up the evidence for the Resurrection, Paul is careful to include the appearances to others.

It might be objected that this appearance to Paul was long after the Ascension of Jesus, and ought not to be classed with the appearances immediately after the Resurrection. My answer is that the most logical mind in the world, that of Paul himself, so classed it. The encounter on the Damascan highway convinced Paul that Jesus was the Son of God, and that He had risen from the dead. That conviction accounts for the greatest moral transformation and mental change of which we have any record.

There are plenty of men who hate Jesus Christ and His Church in the world, today. They write against Him, and speak against

Him, and work against Him. But not even the worst of them hate Him as bitterly and intensely as Paul hated Him. None of them has said as cruel and false and wicked things about Him as Paul said. None of them has tried to destroy his Church with such desperate energy as Paul did. Yet it was this Christ-hater, this Christian-baiter, this Church-destroyer, this man "breathing out threatenings and slaughter" against the Christians, who suddenly became the greatest and most influential friend that Jesus Christ had, or has had, upon the earth; the man whose writings compose the greater part of the New Testament, the man from whom comes the most powerful expression of Christian doctrine, the most beautiful description of the Christian virtues, and the man whose life affords us the grandest example of fellowship with Christ and consecration to the Cross of Christ!

The persecuting Saul of Tarsus changed into Paul, the Apostle of Jesus Christ, is a fact of history. You must face it. You must account for it. What changed him? Paul says it was the appearance of the Risen Christ. Jesus raised from the dead and appearing to Paul is a cause sufficient to account for the great effect, the conversion of Paul. Anything less than that will not account for it. Therefore, the conversion of Paul, and the great life which followed that conversion, bears witness to the fact of the Resurrection.

3. *The Disciples of Jesus.* In the introduction to the book of Acts, Luke says that after His death, Jesus showed Himself alive unto His disciples by "many infallible proofs, being seen of them forty days, and speaking of the things pertaining to the kingdom of God." Our next step then, will be to deal with those appearances and tell what the infallible proofs are. Before I cite them, let me say that Luke, who thus refers to the infallible proofs of the Resurrection, and elsewhere, in his own gospel, gives a careful history of the Resurrection, is recognized as one of the world's most reliable historians. His two books deal with one of the most difficult periods of history, when administration was most complex. Yet although freely mentioning cities, towns and persons, Luke is nowhere found to be in error. Bear that in mind when we come to a statement like this that by many infallible signs Jesus showed Himself after His death unto the disciples.

No one doubts that the four Gospels testify to the fact that

Jesus rose from the dead. Whether or not the authors were mistaken, or were willful deceivers, their narratives tell us that Christ rose again. In these four accounts there are minor differences which at first appear to be discrepancies and contradictions—such differences, in details, as these: John says it was dark when the women came to the tomb; but Mark says the sun was risen. Matthew says they found the grave closed, and Mark an open grave. In one gospel an angel appears; in another two angels; in another a young man; and in a fourth two men. Matthew and John say the women departed in great joy to tell the disciples; but Mark says they were so frightened that they told no one.

While we may be perplexed at these differences as to incidents of the Resurrection, we are grateful that the four records are not exactly the same as to all details. Had they so been, we might be tempted to think there had been collusion and fraud. But if the Gospels were put together by fabricators, why did they not see to it that their lies were in harmony? These differences in the narratives show sincerity and independence on the part of the narrators. If we had all the facts at hand, the apparent discrepancies would no doubt be explained. As it is, they in no way invalidate the witness of the Gospels, for the main thing is not whether it was dark, or at sunrise, whether there were two angels or just one, what the women said or did not say, but did Christ rise up? Was the tomb empty? As to this the Four Gospels are in perfect agreement.

In his *Life of Jesus*, Strauss, who would resolve most of the story of Jesus into myth or delusion, says, "If we are to consider a miracle of so unheard of a description as having actually occurred, it must be proved to us by evidence in such a manner, that the untruth of such evidence would be more difficult to conceive than the reality of that which it was intended to prove." We accept this test and declare that in view of what took place, in view of the establishment of Christianity in the world through a belief in the Resurrection of Jesus, and in view of the history and character of Jesus as given in the Gospels, it would be far more difficult to think that the Gospels are false, than it is to believe that Christ actually rose from the dead. Indeed, if Christ was who the Gospels present Him to be, the Son of God, and told the truth in His predictions, then it would be difficult to believe that He did not rise from the dead. That was the argument of Peter on the day of Pentecost, when he said it was not possible that He should be holden of death.

4. *The Infallibility of the proofs of the Resurrection* is demonstrated by the complete failure to account for the belief in the Resurrection upon any other grounds. All grant the belief in the Resurrection and the part it played in founding the Church. If that belief did not arise out of the fact of the Resurrection, then it must have arisen in some other way. But what way? Let us look now at the different hypotheses which have been advanced to account for the belief in the Resurrection.

a. That the disciples of Jesus stole the body. According to this hypothesis the Resurrection was a gigantic hoax and fraud. The grave was empty, but because the disciples had stolen the body and then spread the rumor that Jesus had risen. That was what the rulers bribed the Roman guards to say: that His disciples came by night and stole the body. They had to account for the tomb being empty, lest the claims of Jesus be confirmed. The thing is too absurd and preposterous to deserve a moment's consideration. It was a theory worthy of the men who first foisted it on the world, the scribes and Pharisees. If this were so, you would have the moral phenomenon of Christianity built on rottenness. The perpetration of such a humbug is not a sufficient explanation of the moral heroism and enthusiasm of the apostles. Do you imagine Peter, and John, and the other disciples suffering persecution and death for the sake of a Christ whom they knew to be dead, and about whom they were lying?

b. That Christ was not dead, but only in a swoon. From time to time this foolish idea is revived. It is pointed out that crucified men sometimes lived for several days. In the cool grotto of Joseph, Jesus revived and, escaping, went back to the city. But this is contrary to the story of the Crucifixion. The soldiers did not give the finishing blow, the breaking of the legs, to Jesus, for He was already dead, but one, just to amuse himself, took a spear and thrust it into His side. In the victim's weakened state, even had He not been dead before, that blow would have proved mortal. Moreover, Pilate, before he set the guard, secured from the rulers a death certificate.

But suppose He had survived the agony of the Cross and the process of embalming, how could He have gotten out of the tomb? How rolled the stone away? And even if this, in some way, had been done, and Jesus had found His way back to the disciples and been nursed back to life, can you conceive of such a Christ inspiring His disciples with heroic faith and courage and making them believe that he was the Son of God? Even Strauss scorned such a theory: "It is impossible that a being who had stolen half-dead out of the sepulchre, who had crept about weak and ill, wanting medical treatment, who required bandaging, strengthening, and indulgence, and who at last yielded to His sufferings, could have given to the disciples the impression that He was the conqueror over death and the grave, the Prince of Life, an impression which lay at the bottom of their future ministry."

c. Hallucination. According to this theory, the disciples did not actually see Jesus risen from the grave, but merely thought they had seen Him. What would you think of a woman who told you that she had seen her deceased husband risen from the grave, that she had talked with him and eaten with him? You would say that long hours of watching and nursing, loss of sleep and wearing grief had produced in the woman's mind an impression favorable to self-deception and hallucination. So it was, we are told, with the disciples of Jesus. Mary, for instance, is recorded as having taken Christ to be the gardener, while the more likely thing is that she took the gardener to be Christ. In the uncertain light of the early morn they were not sure just what they had seen. They wished that Jesus were not dead. They found it hard to believe that He was dead, just as millions of mourners have felt as they stood by the grave of their beloved dead. Their wish was father to their thought—that He was not dead, that He must rise again. Their grief created their dreams, or visions, and their visions created their belief. So the legend arose. Grief gave it wings. So Renan concludes his Life of Jesus: "Had this body been taken away, or did enthusiasm, always credulous, create afterwards the group of narratives by which it was sought to establish faith in the resurrection? In the absence of opposing documents this can never be ascertained. Let us say, however, that the strong imagination of Mary Magdalene played an important part in this circumstance. Divine power of love! Sacred moments in which the passion of one possessed gave to the world a resuscitated God!"

But suppose, now, for the sake of argument, that Jesus had not risen, and that the disciples were the victims of hallucination, through grief, enthusiasm, or whatever you please. Where, then, is the body of Jesus? If the disciples had the body hidden away somewhere, they could hardly be deceived into thinking that Jesus was risen; and if the body was in the tomb, or elsewhere in the custody of the scribes and Pharisees, they would have produced the corpse to prove that the disciples who were preaching Jesus and the Resurrection were a set of liars and impostors. But they could not do this. The best they could do was to finance a lie that the disciples had stolen the body and hid it somewhere.

They found not the body of Jesus! That empty tomb baffles every theory and every hypothesis which would seek to account for the origin of the belief in the Resurrection upon some other ground than that of the fact of the Resurrection. The only theory which explains the empty grave is the theory of the Gospels, the theory that created the Church, that sent men forth to meet the brandished sword, the leaping flame, "the lion's gory mane"; the theory that changed the Christ-hating and Church-persecuting Saul into the great apostle Paul; the theory that transfigures the face of sorrow and sings the lantern of hope in the darkness of the grave; the theory which alone accounts for the rise and spread of Christianity; the theory upon the truth of which rests all our trust for the forgiveness of our sins, all our belief in fellowship now with Christ our Lord and Redeemer, and all our hope of life after death, our own personal survival and the reunion on the fields of eternity with the loved and the lost on the fields of time; the theory upon which rest all the other truths of Christianity; the theory which is the headstone of the corner, holding up the whole glorious structure of the Christian temple; the theory attested by many infallible proofs that on the third day Jesus rose again from the dead, "declared to be the Son of God with power . . . by the resurrection from the dead."

8

Did Christ Ascend into Heaven?

So then after the Lord had spoken unto them, he was received up into heaven, and sat on the right hand of God (Mark 16:19).

The Christian religion is indissolubly linked with four great miracles or manifestations of the Divine power and will for the redemption of mankind. These four miracles are, The Incarnation, or the Son of God becoming the Son of man, the Resurrection, the Ascension into heaven, and His coming again to judge the world. Three of these belong to the history of Christianity; the fourth belongs to the undiscovered territory of the future. It was a momentous day for our planet when the Son of God appeared upon it in the likeness of our flesh. It was a great day for the Christian Church when a cloud received Him out of the sight of men and He vanished from the earth. It will again be a great day for the world when that vanished Christ shall come again in glory.

There is, today, an ever-increasing tendency to dissociate Christianity from its supernatural facts and to try to take and enjoy its great principles and high hopes without regard to the truth of the alleged facts upon which it must stand. But this is impossible. A house must have foundations, and if the foundations be destroyed, the house collapses. We have seen enough of the history of the rejection of the great doctrines of Christianity on the part of those who would, at the same time, take advantage of the hopes and principles of Christianity, to know that after men have rejected the facts upon which the hopes rest, it is exceedingly difficult for them to entertain the hopes. The forgiveness of sins, the triumph of righteousness in the world and the fadeless life beyond the dark cavern of the tomb, inevitably sink and disappear when the facts which inspired these ideas are abandoned.

The fact that we have large groups of Christians, and even an organized church or two, holding to, and proclaiming, these hopes and laws, while at the same time making it clear that they either reject altogether, or regard but lightly the facts of Christian history, need not disturb anyone, for these groups and churches are operating solely on the spiritual capital of the past, and their very existence today in the world is wholly dependent upon the presence in the world of Christian groups and churches who are loyal to the facts of Christianity.

A Great Fact of Christianity

We have now for our discussion one of the great facts of Christianity, the Ascension of Jesus. During the forty days after His Resurrection Jesus remained near, or with, His disciples, appearing unto them now as they walked into the country, now as they were met together on the Lord's Day, and now as they held to their nets in the fishing boats of Galilee, as the mists began to lift from the face of the sea.

There were two reasons why He tarried this long, before He bade the earth and His disciples a final farewell. First, that they might be convinced, beyond all doubt, that He had actually risen from the dead. Without that conviction as to a bodily resurrection of Jesus there could have been no Church and no Christianity. A single appearance was not sufficient. In after ages men might have said that this single appearance was only a pathetic imagination, or an inner vision created by longing hearts. But the many appearances, under many different circumstances, and in many places established the Resurrection so firmly that, as Bishop Gore says, the denial of it from the basis of historical criticism is a "desperate paradox."

If the first reason for this wait of forty days was for the sake of evidence, the second was for the sake of instruction. The ideas of the gospel of redemption which we find so clearly stated and so firmly established in the teachings of the apostles and the Church after the ascension of Jesus, are all found, in germ form, in the sayings of Jesus before the crucifixion. Nevertheless, all must admit the difference between the plain, full statement of Christian truth in the Acts and the Epistles and that which we have in the Gospels. When and where did the disciples so quickly get that full comprehension of the message they were to give to the world? Through the promised coming of the Holy Spirit, undoubtedly; but also through the instruction which they received from Jesus during these forty days.

In one Gospel we are told, for instance, that beginning at Moses and all the prophets Jesus interpreted to them in all the Scriptures the things concerning Himself. In the sermon which Peter preached to the Roman centurion Cornelius, he gives a very complete summary of Christianity as it was preached and established in the world by the apostles. This gospel was, in brief: Jesus as the fulfillment of prophecy, the One through whom men have the remission of sin, and as the Judge of the whole earth; and he adds that Jesus gave them this message about Himself after His resurrection. Those forty days, therefore, were the days when Christian theology arose in its true and divine form, not in the imagination of men, but from the command of Jesus Himself.

But when these ends had been secured, when the faith of the disciples in the Resurrection had been established, and they had been instructed as to what they were to preach, it was no longer expedient for Jesus to remain upon earth. Indeed, it was expedient, as He said, that He should go away from them. Had He remained, where would He have remained? In Jerusalem, Capernaum, Athens, Rome? No, the natural and the necessary step is His disappearance and ascension. "He led them out as far as to Bethany," says Luke; in Acts he says "the mount called Olivet," at the foot of which lay Bethany. Gethsemane also was on the Mount of Olives, and perhaps where our Lord drank the bitter cup of His humiliation and felt most keenly the weight of the world's woe and shame—there He ascended to the glory which He had forsaken at the right hand of God. Lifting His hands in blessing upon them

He was taken from them and "a cloud received him out of their sight." Out of that cloud He has never since appeared, save to the eyes of the dying Stephen, and to the eyes of Paul. Jesus of Nazareth has departed from the earth. His disciples will see Him no more. But now, instead of the sorrow and dismay with which they followed Him to the tomb in the dark eclipse of all their hopes, they return to the city with great joy, there to wait for the equipment of the Holy Spirit.

Heaven Is a Place as Well as a State

What is related here in the Gospels and in Acts is everywhere assumed and stated in the teaching and writings of the apostles. The most familiar statement of the Ascension of Jesus is that He ascended to the right hand of God. Of course, God, being a Spirit, has neither right hand nor left, and such expressions are used in the Bible only to help us hold to the fact, or truth, which is thus symbolized. Yet when Jesus disappeared it was a real disappearance, a real exit from this world, a real entrance into another world. Since the people of that day thought of heaven as some place over their heads, there is no reason why Jesus, in the act of His ascension, should not have accommodated Himself to their supposition and given them a manifestation of a body rising from the earth. Indeed, unless there had been some such real manifestation, it is difficult to understand how they could have become convinced, as they were convinced, that the occasional appearances of Jesus were at an end, and that a new chapter had opened for them.

It is idle to say, and with boasting, that heaven is no more above our heads than it is under our feet, and that the idea of an ascension, while easy for men who had the static and mechanical thought of the heavens, is impossible for us who know that what we point to tonight among the shining stars tomorrow will be under our feet. What the ascension tells us is that Jesus passed from the visible world into the invisible and spiritual world, which is the abiding world.

Where did Jesus go? To what did He ascend? To heaven? But what and where is heaven? Almost half a century ago there appeared a book entitled *The Unseen Universe*, the result of the collaboration of two very distingnished physicists, who happened to be men of Christian faith as well. The chief idea running through the book is that the visible and material world, which we are tempted to regard as being the only universe, is only a temporary thing, the temporary staging and expression of the original and immaterial and invisible universe. Both science and prophecy seem to point to the dissolution and disappearance of this present material universe, when, in the eloquent language of Isaiah, "All the host of heaven shall be dissolved, and the heavens shall be rolled together as a scroll," when

> The cloud-capped towers, the gorgeous palaces,
> The solemn temples, the great globe itself,
> Yea, all which it inherit, shall dissolve;—
> And like this unsubstantial pageant, faded,
> Leave not a wrack behind.

After all, how little we know about the universe which lies within our knowledge and observation, to say nothing of the world beyond, and that little knowledge will certainly not lead us to conclude that this is the only universe. What lies beyond those stars that will shine down tonight? Wing your way from star to star, stand at length on the remotest verge of the physical universe, what can you tell me of that which lies beyond it or around it? The Scriptures do not locate or describe heaven, but when Jesus ascended into heaven to the right hand of God He passed through into a world that is just as real as the world in which we live today.

Christ as Our Intercessor

The chief lessons of the Ascension are not those of celestial geography or topography, but of spiritual and Christian significance. In that invisible world to which Christ has gone the great office of our Lord is that of an intercessor with God for all who in this life believe on Him. Even before His death, Jesus interceded with God for the souls of men. He said He had prayed for His disciples, and especially for Peter, on that last night, that his faith might not fail him; and for all the Twelve, for all Christian believers, past, present, and to come, Jesus prayed in the sublime intercession at the Last Supper. In the subsequent literature of the New Testament this act of intercession appears as the present work of Christ. When He died on Calvary He cried out to heaven and earth and hell, It is finished! It was finished, the great act of sacrifice and redemption, and all else in the future is but the application, or working out, of what was done once for all on the Cross.

The work of Christ as an Intercessor is not a new work of redemption, but His presenting Himself to God as our Redeemer and thereby "modifying the incidence" of the Divine law towards us "Who is even at the right hand of God, who also maketh intercession for us" (Romans 8:34). "He is also able to save them to the uttermost that come unto God by him, seeing he ever liveth to make intercession for them" (Hebrews 7:25). As once in the year, on the great day of atonement, the high priest of Israel, clad in white garments, and with tinkling bell and the blood of sacrifice, passed within the veil to makes intercession for the people, remaining there but a little, Christ, our great High Priest, has passed into the heavens, within the veil, where in the very holy of holies, at the right hand of God Himself, He makes intercession for His people. But does God the Father need to be won or wooed to mercy and benevolence by prayers and offerings? No; the intercession of Jesus is but the demonstration and proclamation, in heaven, of that ground upon which God forgives sin, and restores man to the household of His love.

Every man who is a confessed follower of Jesus Christ has in his behalf the mighty intercession of Jesus with God. In quiet, twilight hours our hearts go yearningly out in the direction of the invisible world, whither our beloved departed have entered, and, sometimes, we wonder how near they are to us, or what offices they may perform in our behalf. Do they hold us in full survey and compass us about as a cloud of witnesses? Do they rejoice when they behold us saying to temptation, "Get thee behind me"? And do they know sadness and dismay and fear when they behold us, in spite of their prayers and whatever interventions are granted unto them, forsake the good and choose death rather than life? Perhaps so. We like to think so.

What we do know is that One who knows us better than our nearest and our dearest— One who was tempted in all points like as we are, yet without sin, One who is touched with a feeling of our daily and hourly infirmities, Jesus the Creator of the world, Who died on the Cross, Who rose again the third day, Who ascended into heaven and sits at the right hand of God the Father Almighty—prays for us. Oh, if the recollection that some wife or little child, or blessed mother or father, or true friend, now prays for us that we may be kept from the evil way, or that our faith may not fail us, and if the recollection of the prayers that we, ourselves, out of a pure heart once offered unto God for ourselves—if the thought of these intercessions helps and strengthens and purifies, so that hearts are brave again and arms are strong, how much more will it help us to remember that Christ ever lives to make intercession for us!

The Heavenly Possibilities of Human Nature

Jesus came down from heaven as the Eternal Son of the Father, but when He went back to the seat of honor and of glory at God's right hand, He took with Him our own nature. He returned to His Father as God-man. That human nature which He assumed in Bethlehem's cradle He never relinquished or laid aside. In that nature He met the assaults of the Tempter in the desert; in that nature, in busy highway or green hillside or by the unsleeping sea, He spoke the message of the Kingdom; in that nature He drank Gethsemane's cup and entered into the darkness of death on Calvary; in that nature He rose again and appeared unto His disciples; and in that same body, no longer now the body of humiliation, but the body of His glory, He ascended into the heavens. Forever God and Man, He reigns in heaven. It was our nature, in everything but its sin, that sat down at the right hand of God.

In the ascended humanity of Jesus we behold our destiny, the true destiny of man. In our present weakness, and ignorance, and frailty, it seems too grand a destiny, an end and consummation impossible for us. But the same power that raised and exalted Him, will raise and exalt us too, for He shall "change our vile body that it may be fashioned like unto his glorious body, according to the working whereby he is able ever to subdue all things unto himself." "Man is but a reed, the frailest thing in nature. An exhalation, a drop of water, suffices to destroy him."

Yet for Him there is the seat of glory. "What is man that thou art mindful of him? and the son of man that thou visitest him? For thou hast made him a little lower than the angels." In that state of glory in the life to come redeemed man will be a little higher than the angels, how much higher than the angels none can tell, but certainly higher, for every redeemed being who has passed through the furnace of the sins and trials of this world and been found by Christ, must be higher than an unfallen being.

When the weariness of gathering years creeps upon you, or the fatigue of sickness and disease, or a thick, cold fog of loneliness, or when present temptations assail you, or the memory of past sins burns you like an acid flame, then lift up your eyes unto the heavens, and see what man was made for and what man is capable of, and live for that chief end of man's life.

The Victory of the Church and the Reign of Righteousness

The suffering, humiliated, and rejected Christ is now the exalted and glorified Christ. He is at the right hand of power. The pierced hand rules the world. We look about us, today, and see little evidence of the triumph of Christ and His Church. We behold a Church distressed with Christ-denying heresies and torn with wide and bitter schisms. We behold a world to which Christ gave His law of love and justice—peace on earth and good will to men—ripped apart with a legion of devils of greed, and lust, and hate, and violence, and the cloud about His throne is denser and colder by far than that which one day on Olivet's slopes received Him out of His disciples' sight. Where are the signs of His coming? Where are the conquests of His empire?

> Our Lord is still rejected
>   And by this world disowned;
> By the many still neglected
>   And by the few enthroned.

But this rejected Christ holds the helm of the universe as He sits at God's right hand. When He ascended on high, He took captivity captive. All those forces, and powers, and persons, which by their successful stratagems had held men in captivity, and which appear to hold men in captivity now, in reality have had their spoils wrested from them, and themselves have been made captive. The walls of Satan's fortress have been sapped and its foundations undermined; they wait only for the touch of the Captain of our Salvation to bring them down in ruins. In *The Four Horsemen of the Apocalypse*, the Russian sage and prophet, looking upon the ravages of war, despairs of the death of the Beast. The Beast, he says, never dies. He is the eternal companion of man. He hides spouting blood for fifty or a hundred years, but eventually he reappears. But Christianity has a different horoscope for the world. The Beast has received his fatal wound. Both Death and Hell will be cast into the lake of fire. Christ must reign till He has put all enemies under His feet. "Affairs on this earth may not proceed in a train agreeable to our views and expectations; but it will repress every murmur and every wish for a different order to reflect that He presides over them, who is the Patron of truth and righteousness."

When Julian the Apostate, who sought to light again the fires on the altars of the pagan gods, and destroy Christianity, was on the march with his army in the campaign against Persia, in the year 363, one of the soldiers of his army said to a Christian who was being abused by the soldiery, "Where is your carpenter now?" "He is making a coffin for your emperor," was the reply of the Christian. A few months afterwards, Julian received a mortal wound in battle. The rumor spread through the army that the wound was inflicted by a Christian soldier in the ranks of the Roman army, and according to the story of Theoderet, Julian, realizing that his death was at hand, dipped his hand in the blood of his wound and threw the blood towards heaven, exclaiming as he did so, "Thou hast conquered, O Galilaean!" Yes, the Carpenter of Nazareth, exalted to the right hand of God, is making a coffin for all the kings and kingdoms of this world. One by one they flourish, and are gone. But Christ's is an everlasting kingdom. All that is not obedient to Him, and subject to Him, shall perish. That alone endures which belongs to Him.

9

Will Christ Come Again?

Till he come (1 Cor. 11:26).

The last that "the world" saw of Jesus Christ was when He hung dead upon the Cross at Calvary. But His disciples declared that the dead Jesus rose from the grave and appeared unto them, during a period of forty days showing Himself alive by many infallible proofs. At the end of that time He ascended into heaven and a cloud received Him out of their sight. But, instead of grieving and despairing because they saw Him no more, the disciples returned to Jerusalem with great joy and were continually in the temple praising God. What was the secret of that joy? How strange that these disciples should rejoice when their Lord is taken from them! The secret of their joy was that they expected Him to return.

Before His death, and perhaps between His resurrection and His ascension, Jesus had instructed the disciples as to His return to the earth. Still, it is one thing to receive instruction, another thing to act upon it. They were gazing steadfastly up into heaven, thinking we hardly know what, as they looked upon the cloud which had received their Lord out of their sight, when two men robed in white stood by them and said, "Ye men of Galilee, why stand ye gazing up into heaven? this same Jesus, which is taken up from you into heaven, shall so come in like manner as ye have seen him go into heaven."

God knows when to speak to His children and what to speak. His angels come when our hearts need to hear their message. With that great assurance ringing in their ears, the disciples returned to Jerusalem filled with joy and hope. In a few days the Holy Spirit was poured out upon them, and the Christian Church commenced its work in the world.

The promise that our Lord will come again occupies such a place in Christian revelation that to ask the question, Will Christ come again? amounts to saying, Is the New Testament reliable? or, Is Christianity true? If Christ is not coming again, then a negative answer must be given to both these questions. As Canon Liddon, one of the greatest preachers of his time, once put it when preaching in St. Paul's: "If Christ is not coming back in glory, then let us turn the key in the west door of this cathedral." Paul said that if Christ were not risen, the preaching of Christianity was foolishness. So we may say that if Christ is not coming again in glory, it is folly to preach Christianity, because we are preaching what is not true.

In popular speech this teaching of the New Testament is referred to as the "second" coming of Christ, and the word "second" is used to differentiate between the coming of Christ in glory and His coming in humility when He was born of the Virgin Mary at Bethlehem. But the Bible nowhere speaks of a "second coming." There, it is always the "coming," or the "presence" of the Lord.

The event was of so great significance that it stood by itself in meaning and in glory. In this day, when so many Christians appear never to have heard of the doctrine, or who, if they have, regard it as something which has no meaning for their everyday life, it may not be out of place to say that the belief in the Coming of the Lord is presented to us in the sacraments, the offices, the prayers and the creeds of the holy, universal Church. In the Lord's Prayer when we say "Thy Kingdom come," it is the coming of the Lord for which we pray. In the Apostles' Creed we confess that He will come to judge the quick and the dead.

Never a Christian is buried but the minister refers in the committal service to the Coming of Christ, for he says, "Earth to earth, ashes to ashes, dust to dust. Looking for the resurrection of the dead and the life of the world to come through our Lord Jesus

Christ, at whose appearing in glorious majesty, the earth and the sea shall give up their dead, and the mortal bodies of them that sleep in Him shall be changed and made like to His own glorious body." And never a celebration of the Lord's Supper is held but the officiating minister, or priest, gives the bread and the wine to the people, repeating as he does so the words of Paul: "For as oft as ye eat this bread and drink this cup ye do show forth the Lord's death till he come." All our worship, all our working, all our praying, looks forward to that great day when He shall come.

Because it is an event which belongs to the future, thus being in contrast with the other three great miracles of Christianity, the Incarnation, the Resurrection and the Ascension, which all belong to the past, to history, the belief in the Coming of the Lord has suffered much at the hands of enthusiasts, with the result that it has been given a place which the Scriptures do not give to it, to the end that many, offended with these extravagances, have turned from it altogether. But the abuse of the doctrine on the one hand, and the total neglect of it on the other, is no reason why Christian believers should not be instructed concerning it, and receive comfort and inspiration from it.

It would be a tragedy if in this day, when rationalism and modernism are taking the mask from their faces and revealing themselves as the enemies of our Lord, His disciples should fall to quarreling among themselves as to the time, and the order of the Coming of the Lord, instead of marching shoulder to shoulder against the common foe. The menace of unbelief ought to unite in one grand army believing men and women of all denominations and all Christian Churches. I will therefore purposely avoid those subjects in connection with the Coming of Christ about which contentions have arisen, and over which Christian people have divided themselves according to their favorite interpretation, and deal with those truths of the Coming of our Lord about which all Christians are in agreement. That great agreement as to the cardinal facts is far more significant than any disagreement as to minor facts, such as the place that a millennium takes in the Coming of the Lord, or whether the final kingdom of peace and beauty is to be here on this earth or elsewhere. What I shall try to do, therefore, is to state the reasons for the belief in the Coming of the Lord, and show why it is that for long centuries the Christian

Church has confessed together, "From thence He shall come to judge the quick and the dead."

We Believe Christ Will Come Again Because Christ Said So

If a true Christian is convinced that Jesus said He would come again, that is sufficient for him. He needs no further evidence. The moral authority and infallibility of Jesus is involved in this question as to His return to judge the quick and the dead. To see how repeatedly and unmistakably Jesus declared that He would come again, all that is necessary is to take the Four Gospels and read through them. Christ there says that He will come again in glory with His angels. This Coming will be visible to all, like lightning coming out of the east and shining to the west. In terms of tremendous imagery, an extinguished sun, a dimmed moon, stars falling from heaven, the powers of heaven and earth shaken, the whole Universe in convulsion, He describes the conditions which shall exist when the Son of man comes. Yet He also says the time of His coming is unpredictable and unexpected. It will overtake humanity as the deluge in the days of Noah and as a thief in the night. At such an hour as men think not, He will come. In His great prophetic discourse, as recorded in the last part of Matthew's Gospel, He foretells also the destruction of Jerusalem and the great tribulation which would overtake the Jews at that time. But there is also in His mind a greater calamity and judgment, and those near events of God's judgments are but the faint rumblings of the storm which is to come.

The great parables, such as The Wise and Foolish Virgins, The Talents, The Husbandmen who slew the Heir of the Lord of the Vineyard, and The Pounds, however rich and imaginative the homiletic lessons which preachers draw from them, all have for their one great lesson, the unexpectedness, the suddenness, the blessings and the judgments of Christ's Coming again. In His last, tender address to His disciples, Jesus comforted them with the promise of the coming of the Comforter, the Holy Spirit. But beyond that was the definite assurance that He would come again and receive them unto Himself. After His resurrection, when Peter wanted to know what was to be the fate of John, Jesus told him that it was his duty to follow his Lord regardless of what happened to John: "If I will that he tarry till I come, what is that to thee? Follow thou me."

If we can be sure of anything about Jesus, we can be sure that He said He would come again to this earth, visibly, in glory, accompanied by the heavenly beings, and at a time of terrible distress and suffering among men and nations. If Christ is not coming again, then His moral authority is destroyed and we cannot worship Him as God. The theory that this apocalyptic teaching was added by some of the Christian disciples who had been accustomed to that sort of literature among the Jews, is not satisfactory. Just as there is no such person as a Jesus who was not born of the Virgin Mary, and who did not work miracles, so there is no such person as a Jesus who did not declare, in the most explicit terms, that He would come again.

We Believe That Christ Will Come Again Because the Apostles Said He Would

Luke commences his history of the Christian Church by reporting what the angels said to the disciples at the Ascension, that Jesus would come in like manner as they had seen Him go. The echo of that promise is heard in every sermon preached by the apostles. They are men whose backs are to the world and whose faces are turned towards the Coming of the Lord. Because He is coming, they are encouraged to endure persecution and affliction; because He is coming, they are enjoined to live godly, sober and righteous lives; and because He is coming, and will bring the Christian dead with Him, they are bidden to comfort their broken hearts in time of sorrow and bereavement.

One has counted as many as three hundred and eighteen passages in the New Testament which declare, or reflect, the hope of the Coming of the Lord. If you were to take your New Testament and blot out all the passages which tell of the Coming of the Lord, you would have left in your hands a strange-looking book. It would be so filled with lacunae as to be practically unintelligible.

To the most careless reader of the New Testament it is evident that the driving power of the apostolic Church was the belief held by those who formed it that Christ was coming back to earth, and the hope that He was coming in their own day, before they died.

Give to the apostles and the Christian believers the hope of the appearing of the Lord Jesus Christ, and you can account for their incomparable labors and their flaming love, and their mighty achievement. Deny that they had that belief, and you have no explanation of what they endured and what they accomplished. Still further, to say that they did have the belief, but that they were mistaken, and that Christ will never come, is to say that the Christian religion, with all its conquests and all its beneficent influences, is to be traced back to a colossal delusion.

We Believe That Christ Will come Again Because We Believe in the Reign of the Righteous

Both common sense and experience forbid us to think that the reign of righteousness, the rule of God upon earth, will ever be established except through the Coming of Christ. Before stating the reasons for this, it will help us in our thought of the Coming of the Lord if we summarize in a few sentences what the New Testament teaches us about the concomitants of the great event, the things which shall take place, before, at the time, and after the Advent of Christ.

Without entering upon any disputed territory, we may say that most Christians believe that before Christ comes the world must be evangelized. This Gospel of the Kingdom shall be preached in all the world for a witness unto all nations: and then shall the end come. Either before or after the Coming of Christ the Jews will accept Christ as the Messiah and, as Paul said, all Israel shall be saved. Before He comes there shall be wars and rumors of war, with convulsions in both the political and the physical world. Then comes a period of tribulation when Christ's people shall be persecuted, when false prophets shall lead men astray, and the love of many shall wax cold. During that time there shall be many false rumors that Christ is come, and false prophets shall work great signs and wonders and shall say, "Lo, here is the Christ." This fearful period God in His mercy shall shorten.

Then, with fearful signs in heaven and on earth, with distress on land and on sea, the Son of Man shall come in glory. To this picture of Christ, Paul adds the information about a great apostasy in the Christian Church, and the manifestation of Antichrist, or the Man of Sin. The endless speculations as to Antichrist have only darkened counsel without knowledge. But it is clear from both the words of Jesus and of Paul that this evil is to come to a fearful climax in some person, or institution, which will arrogate to itself power and worship. This power of wickedness Christ shall destroy at His Coming.

At the return of our Lord the dead are to be raised up. All who are in the grave shall hear His voice. Christianity foretells not merely the survival of the human spirit, but the resurrection and the transformation of the body. But that final state is not possible until Christ comes again, for it is at His coming that the dead shall be raised up. Hence the great emphasis which the apostles place on the Coming of the Lord as a doctrine of comfort for the sorrowing. "As in Adam all die, so in Christ shall all be made alive. But every man in his own order: Christ the first fruits; afterward they that are Christ's at his coming." "The Lord himself shall descend from heaven with a shout, with the voice of the archangel, and with the trump of God, and the dead in Christ shall rise first."

After the resurrection of the dead comes the great scene of judgment. The small and the great stand before God. In Christ's picture of the judgment all nations are gathered before Him and given their final destiny, some to everlasting punishment, and some to everlasting joy in the kingdom of God. This world and the order of this world comes to an end. "Then cometh the end when he shall deliver up the Kingdom to God, even the Father, that God may be all in all." There will be a new heaven and a new earth. In this new heaven and new earth sin, war, lust, hate, strife, sorrow, pain, and death will not exist. "There shall be no more curse; but the throne of God and of the Lamb shall be in it; and his servants shall serve him; and they shall see his face; and his name shall be in their foreheads. And there shall be no night there; and they need no candle neither light of the sun! for the Lord God giveth them light; and they shall reign for ever and ever." Is it to be a kingdom of beauty and glory on some other sphere? Or is it to be established here upon this earth? Men differ as to the place; but there is perfect agreement as to the state of this Kingdom of God, this great and glorious end, when God shall be all and in all.

The important thing to keep in mind is the end, that state of perfection which the Bible pictures as established after the Coming of the Lord. The hope which beats within the breast of man has ever pictured a great and a good end to the long process of history.

> There is something here
> Unfathomed by the cynic's sneer;
> Something that gives our feeble light
> A high immunity from Night.
>
> A conscience more divine than we,
> A gladness fed on secret tears;
> A vexing, forward reaching sense
> Of some more noble permanence;
> A light across the sea,
> Which haunts the soul and will not let it be,
> Still beaconing from the heights of undegenerate years.

But how is this kingdom of perfection to come in? In answer to this great question—it is a question which no man who has risen to the dignity of his nature will fail to ask himself—men divide themselves into two groups. First, there are those who believe that through a process of natural evolution the world will come to perfection. They point to the progress which humanity has already made, and remind us that in this vast undertaking one day is as a thousand years and a thousand years as one day. By and by, the ape and the tiger will die out of man's nature. All evils will disappear and righteousness shall cover the earth as the waters cover the sea.

We are not to expect great convulsions or cataclysms, and instead of a great falling away or recession in the tide of progress, the Kingdom of God will come gradually in until at length the world reaches that "one far-off, divine event towards which the whole creation moves." There is a school of thought which joins in this altogether unscriptural expectation. Thus Dr. Shailer Mathews said: "To bring Jesus into the control of human affairs is the real coming of the kingdom of God upon earth. This is what the pictures and the apocalyptic symbols used by the early Christians really meant. This is the real coming of Christ." In like manner, Dr. Harry Emerson Fosdick describes a body of belief which said, "when they say Christ is coming, mean that slowly it may be, but surely, His will and principles will be worked out by God's grace in human life and institutions, until He shall see of the travail of his soul and be satisfied!" Thus, by the slow working out of forces now resident in human society, the world will be transformed.

This belief in the inevitable progress of human society towards perfection is not nearly so strong as it once was, and that rosy confidence has, in many quarters, given way to cynical despair. Even from the standpoint of the scientist, men are not so sure that we move ever towards a goal of perfection. Fabre, the great French entomologist, sees no promise of an evolution to perfection: "The abolition of slavery and the education of woman: these are the two enormous strides upon the path of moral progress.—To what an ideal height will this process of evolution lead mankind? To no very magnificent height it is to be feared. We are afflicted by an indelible taint, a sort of original sin, a state of things with which we have nothing to do. We are made after a certain pattern and we can do nothing to change ourselves. We are marked with the mark of the beast, the taint of the belly, the inexhaustible source of bestiality."

Not only is there nothing in the history of the world, or in the state of the world, today, which warrants the expectation of this natural evolution to perfection—for evil is ever strong, and forces of destruction are ever withstanding the forces of construction—but even if by a process of evolution the moral nature of humanity should in some way be transformed, still, this perfect creature would be left in an imperfect world, for there is nothing in purely moral forces and powers which can destroy the natural enemies of man and make this earth a perfect platform for his existence. As Father Tyrrell put it: "Shall progress ever wipe away the tears from all eyes? Shall it ever extinguish love, and pride, and ambition, and all the griefs attendant in their train? Prolong life as it will, can progress conquer death with its terrors for the dying, its tears for the surviving? Can it ever control the earthquake, the tempest, the lightning, the cruelties of a nature indifferent to the lot of man?"

Instead of this process of natural evolution, which can lead humanity to no goal of happiness, but only through the endless and monotonous cycles of the past, the Christian revelation of the

Coming of the Lord tells us of a new creature in a new heaven and a new earth. This change will be brought about through no natural, inevitable growth, but through the mighty intervention of Christ, and the supersession of the present order. In preparation for this change the long ages of Christian teaching, and preaching, and moral education are to play their part. The good wheat is to grow until the harvest. But also the evil tares. We are to fight against evil and witness for Christ, but we are not to expect that the evil will disappear, or be finally separated from the good, until the harvest, that is, until Christ comes. That was the meaning of His profound saying: "So is the kingdom of God, as if a man should cast seed into the ground; and should sleep and rise night and day, and the seed should spring and grow up; he knoweth not how; for the earth bringeth forth fruit of herself; first the blade, then the ear, and after that the full corn in the ear. But when the fruit is brought forth immediately he putteth in the sickle, because the harvest is come."

The tremendous figures employed by Jesus, a quenched sun, a faded moon, and falling stars, mean what they may, certainly do not lead us to expect any such thing as a gradual ripening of the world into perfection. The world will be made perfect, but only when God brings human history to a climax with the mighty intervention of Christ, when He shall come to judge the quick and the dead. This dramatic, cataclysmal climax to human history is in keeping with every portion of the Christian revelation and every instinct of the human mind. If Christ's Church has been in this world to witness and preach the truth, to toil and suffer for the truth, then it is only right and natural that there should be some crowning vindication of that to which the Church has witnessed—the Kingdom of God. In the words of Bishop Gore in his book, *Belief in Christ*, "His judgment upon men and things will be shown to be the final judgment and the judgment of God. And this Day, like all the partial and preparatory 'days of judgment,' will speak the divine doom on all the corrupt civilizations and godless and inhuman forms of power and civilization and institutions of cruelty and lust, and on all rebels against God and right, only not partially and locally, but universally, in the whole created world."

The disciples asked Jesus a very sensible question when they said, "What shall be the sign of thy coming and the end of the world?" They linked His coming with the termination of the present order. Common sense tells us that the present order must come to an end. "Then cometh the end" is as necessary to human thinking as "In the beginning." We cannot think either that things are to go on forever as they are, this ceaseless ebb and flow of good and evil, nor can we think that an inevitable and irresistible law of progress will transform either the moral nature of man himself or the physical platform on which his life is lived. Christianity alone, with the promise of the Coming of the Lord, when all things shall be made new, tells us how the end is to be reached.

As the Coming of the Lord is the only means for the overthrow of the powers of evil and the vindication of the right and the establishment of truth and justice, so also it is only by the Coming of the Lord that we have a provision made for the uniting of all Christ's followers in one vast and unbroken family. Suppose the world should at length ripen into perfection. Would that be all that our hearts desire? If the world were perfected tomorrow, would your heart, my heart, have all that it craves? No; you would still wish for reunion with the beloved dead. Any consummation of the human drama which satisfies the heart must be one which unites all true believers with one another and with Christ. Does any evolutionist suppose that death is going to be *evolved* out of existence? Will human progress abolish the separation of death? Even if every man on earth were a believer in Christ, still there would always be a wall of separation between the living believers in Christ and the departed generations of faith. Faith unites us, and yet we are conscious of the division of time and death.

> One family we dwell in Him,
> One church above, beneath.
> Though now divided by the stream,
> The narrow stream of death.
>
> One army of the Living God,
> To His command we bow.
> Part of His Host have crossed the flood,
> And part are crossing now.

That grand hymn of Wesley's is well enough for this world. But who wants to sing that song always? Who wants to acknowledge and face the fact that the Church of Jesus Christ is divided by the stream of death? No; death itself must be abolished, and all believers united forever in one home and about one common Lord and Christ. Therefore we pray, "Even so come, Lord Jesus!" With the answer to that prayer, human history will come to an end, and God shall be all and in all.

10

JESUS AND PAUL—DO THEY DIFFER?

I have appeared unto thee to appoint thee a minister and a witness both of things wherein thou hast seen me, and of the things wherein I will appear unto thee (Acts 26:16).

One of the most striking recommendations of the Christian religion is the great variety of attacks which have been made upon it in order to discredit it. From every direction some attack has been launched against the citadel of Christian faith only to be hurled back, beaten and baffled. One army has assailed its prophecies and predictions; another its miracles; another the Old Testament, and another the New Testament; another the miraculous and supernatural, so inextricably wound up with Christianity; another the historicity of its Founder; another His deity; another His miraculous entry into the world; another His resurrection from the dead; another His atoning, substitutionary and expiatory death upon the Cross; another His coming again to judge the world.

Today, one of the favorite modes of attack is to try to create the impression of a discrepancy and a disharmony between Jesus and His greatest apostle, Paul. The Christian religion, we are told, comes from Jesus, but Christian theology comes from Paul. The Christian Church is founded, not upon the teachings of Jesus, but upon the theology of Paul, who took the simple story of Jesus as we have it in the Gospels, and grafted upon it a mass of speculative doctrines about sin, and salvation, and faith, which Jesus Himself never taught. The Peasant-Teacher of Galilee, Paul transformed into a Great High Priest Who offers Himself upon the altar as a sacrifice for the sin of the world. Thus, at the very beginning, we are told, Paul threw the Church off the right track, and the first necessity is to rid ourselves of his influence, abandon his doctrines, and go back to Jesus.

This alleged disagreement between Jesus and Paul was thus stated by Dr. Vedder in his book, *The Fundamentals of Christianity*: "That Jesus of Nazareth spent His public life in giving to the Twelve a teaching that He declared to be the Way of Life; and that He had no sooner left the world than from His state of glory He straightway deputed another man to be His mouthpiece and chief accredited organ; and that through this new mouthpiece He proceeded to set aside the chief part of what He had taught during His lifetime, substituting for its simple ethics a complicated group of theological speculations, so as to make a system of theology the gospel, instead of a proclamation of the Kingdom of God—this is a hypothesis so fantastic, so lacking in all elements of credibility, that one marvels how it could find a sane advocate anywhere. Who can credit that the Heavenly Christ taught through Paul something so different from what the earthly Jesus taught the Twelve?— It is a historical fact, of course, that the entire Church of the following centuries proceeded to substitute Paul for Jesus, as the authoritative teacher of Christianity.—Paul's teaching was quietly put in the place of the teaching of Jesus. Not one of the great theologians of the Church—Athanasius, Augustine, Anselm, Aquinas, Melancthon, Calvin—drew any considerable part of his doctrine from the words of Jesus. All, without exception, Catholic or Protestant, are expounders of Paul."

The one thing which we can commend in this extraordinary arraignment of Christian doctrine is that instead of attacking, as formerly has been the custom, the Westminster Confession of Faith, or the writings of Calvin, and Luther, and Augustine, this author only acknowledges that the fountain from which these men drew their teaching was Paul. According to this writer, and others of the Modernist school, Paul was badly mistaken, and his teachings have nothing in common with those of Jesus. Nevertheless, we are indebted to these gentlemen for making the issue so clear cut, no longer obscuring it with angry talk about creeds and Calvin and Augustine and theologians, but saying plainly that Paul is the source of Christian theology, and that Jesus and Paul cannot be reconciled.

Many years ago Renan, in the closing chapter of his *Life of St. Paul*, wrote in a similar vein: "After having been for three centuries, thanks to orthodox Protestantism, the Christian teacher *par excellence*, Paul sees in our day his reign drawing to a close. Jesus, on the contrary, lives more than ever. It is no longer the Epistle to the Romans which is the Resume of Christianity—it is the Sermon on the Mount. True Christianity, which will last forever, comes from the Gospels, not from the Epistles of Paul. The writings of Paul have been a danger and a hidden rock, the causes of the principal defects of Christian theology. Paul is the father of the subtle Augustine, of the fierce theology which damns and predestinates to damnation.—Jesus is the father of all those who seek repose of their souls in dreams of the ideal."

Since the ideas of Paul do undoubtedly dominate Christian theology, and since his writings constitute the major portion of the New Testament, which all Christians take as the rule of their faith, the charge that Paul differs from Jesus, teaching what Jesus did not, and would not teach, is a very serious one, and worthy of our careful examination. It will therefore be our purpose to show, upon the basis of a comparison of the teachings of Jesus with the teachings of Paul, that this charge is entirely groundless, that Jesus and Paul are in complete harmony, and that Paul teaches nothing which Jesus did not teach and authorized him to teach.

Since the complaint is made against Paul, that he had added to the teachings of Jesus, thus departing from the original rule of faith, instead of taking first the teachings of Jesus and then seeing if Paul agrees or disagrees with them, we shall take first the teachings of Paul and see whether or not Jesus taught the same thing. The charge is not that what you find in Jesus you cannot find in Paul, but that what is found in Paul cannot be found in Jesus.

The Testimony of Paul and the First Apostles

Before taking up that examination and comparison it ought to be said that Paul's own testimony as to the source of his teaching must be given consideration. Paul, whether false or true, was a very clear-headed man, and he says in the most unmistakable language that he got the gospel which he preached from Jesus Himself. In his threefold account of his conversion on the way to Damascus, he represents Christ as saying that He has chosen Paul to bear witness to Him and preach His gospel among the nations. Paul certainly never had any idea that he was preaching anything except what Jesus authorized him to preach. In another place he says he was not taught the gospel he was preaching, neither did he receive it of man, but by a revelation of Jesus Christ. Nowhere in all the many writings of Paul will one find a single passage which would lead one to believe that he thinks of his gospel as differing in the least respect from the Gospel of the Lord Jesus Christ.

Furthermore, not only was Paul unconscious of any innovation in his teachings about Christianity, but so also were the other apostles who had been with Jesus in the flesh and had heard Him teach, and had seen Him in the resurrection, and would, therefore, have been in a position to detect anything in Paul which was in excess of, or contradictory to, what Jesus had taught. The Churches in Judea, Paul says, when they heard the tremendous tidings, "He that once persecuted us now preacheth the faith of which he once made havoc," "glorified God in me." In other words, Paul's preaching, as it was reported to the Christians in Jerusalem, was a full proclamation of Jesus Christ such as they were familiar with.

When Paul came to Jerusalem and carefully laid before them what he was preaching, the three great leaders of the Church, Peter, James and John, gave Paul the right hand of fellowship and bade him Godspeed in his mission to the Gentiles. In his charge that the early Church substituted Paul, the speculative theologian, for Jesus, the ethical teacher, Dr. Vedder says they did it "without consciousness of what they were doing." He could not say anything else, for nowhere in the New Testament, or in the writings of the early Christian Church, is there the least intimation that what Paul taught was different from what Jesus taught. The strange, the unaccountable, thing is that it should have been reserved for men today to discover that there is an unbridgeable gulf between Jesus and Paul.

As we commence our examination and comparison, then, of the

teachings of Jesus and Paul, let us bear in mind that neither Paul himself, nor his contemporaries, nor the Christians of successive centuries of Church history betray the least consciousness of a difference between the Gospel as Jesus preached it and the Gospel as Paul preached it, and since the establishment of Christianity in the European world was, through the providence of God, largely the work of one man, Paul, to say that Paul differs from Jesus as to the meaning of the Gospel amounts to saying that the Christian Church was founded upon a colossal and unaccountable mistake. People then, and through the ages, thought that what Paul was preaching was the Gospel of Jesus Christ, the Son of God. But now, that is discovered to have been a huge blunder.

The Person of Jesus

Paul and Jesus both teach the same thing as to the rank of Jesus. When Paul was struck down on the Damascus highway, he said, in reply to the words of Jesus, "Saul, Saul, why persecutest thou me?" "Who art thou, Lord?" The Voice answered, "I am Jesus of Nazareth, whom thou persecutest." At this, the beginning of their relationship, Jesus did not apply to Himself any of the mighty titles which He rightly could use, the Messiah, the Christ, the Son of God, but simply introduced Himself to Paul as the historical Jesus of Nazareth. That historic humanity of Jesus is common, then, to both Jesus and Paul. If Jesus had said, "I am the Messiah, I am the Son of God," Paul might have answered that it was not such an one that he was persecuting, but Jesus of Nazareth, who claimed to be the Son of God and the Messiah. It is thus the historic Jesus of the Gospels, born at Bethlehem, and brought up at Nazareth, who appeared unto Paul on the road to Damascus.

Paul, in his writings, makes few references to the earthly life of Jesus, though these few references suggest a full knowledge of the facts. His great interest is in the Gospel which came through that historic Jesus of Nazareth. When he had been converted, the first thing Paul did was to preach that Jesus was the Son of God. "And straightway in the synagogues, he proclaimed Jesus that He is the Son of God."

Paul had hated and persecuted Jesus for the same reason that the scribes and Pharisees had persecuted Him—because He claimed to be the Son of God. Now, a converted man, he turns around and preaches that Jesus is the Son of God. In one passage (Rom. 9:5), Paul definitely calls Christ "God, blessed for ever." He applies to Jesus the awful name of "Lord"; almost always it is the "Lord Jesus Christ"; and he applies to Jesus passages from the Greek translation of the Old Testament where "Lord" is used to translate the Holy Name of the God of Israel. Repeatedly also Paul calls Jesus the Son of God (Gal. 4:4,5; Rom. 5:8-10; 8:31, 32). In giving an account of the source of his gospel, Paul says he did not receive it of man but through Jesus Christ. He therefore differentiates between Jesus of Nazareth and mankind. When he went into the synagogues the burden of Paul's preaching was to prove that Jesus was the Christ, the Messiah. Not only does he apply to Jesus these high titles, Son of God, Messiah, God, but he attributes to Jesus power and office which can belong only to God. Through Him and unto Him all things have been created. (Col. 1:16.)

The Jesus of Paul is omnipotent, for He is able to "subdue even all things unto himself." He was preexistent, for God sent Him into the world in the fulness of time, and being in the form of God He humbled Himself and took the form of man. He is the searcher of all hearts and the great judge before whom all men must stand and give account, "for we must all stand before the judgment seat of Christ."

This, then, is Paul's belief about the Jesus of Nazareth who appeared unto him on the road to Damascus, and reversed all his thinking and all his living. He is God's Son incarnate, manifest in the flesh; He is the Christ, the Messiah, the Creator of the worlds, the judge of all the earth, "God over all, blessed forever." He is the supernatural, stupendous Person whom Paul loved and followed, and whom he preached throughout the world.

When we turn back to the Gospels and compare the Christ of Paul with the Jesus of the Gospel narratives we find that they are identical. Paul claimed nothing for Jesus that Jesus did not claim for Himself. Jesus claimed pre-existence, infallibility, Omnipotence, omnipresence, the right to judge men and determine their destiny; and not only did He claim these divine attributes, and prove His right to them by His miracles, but He definitely said that He was the Messiah, the Christ, and the Son of God, and was put to death because He made this awful claim. The Jesus, then, of Paul, is the same as the Jesus of the Gospels.

The Teachings of Jesus and Paul

Space does not permit us to go at length into the teachings of Paul, comparing them with the teachings of Jesus. But I shall mention some of the salient features. No one can read Paul's letters without being impressed with the fact that he believed that the great enemy of the Kingdom of God was the kingdom of darkness and the prince of that kingdom, Satan, the devil, the tempter, the evil one, the god of this age. He declares that our chief warfare as Christians is not with flesh and blood and the visible powers of this world, but with "principalities, the dominions, the world rulers of darkness, the spiritual forces of wickedness." We turn back to the Gospels and we find that Jesus taught precisely the same thing. In the narratives of the Temptation, which could have come from Jesus only, Jesus prepares Himself for His redemptive mission by the solitary struggle with Satan in the wilderness. He said that when He had bound the strong man He would then spoil the goods of his house. The triumph of His Gospel He likened to the fall of Satan from heaven. His disciples, notably Peter, He warned against the temptations of Satan, saying that he desired to have them that he might sift them as wheat. The bitter and wicked opposition to Him on the part of the leaders and rulers of the people He attributed to the influence of Satan. Both Paul and Jesus taught that there are evil spirits warring against the souls of men, and that over against the Kingdom of God stands the kingdom of darkness.

Paul was a great theologian, but he was also what they call today a great "ethical" teacher. In a Gentile civilization which had sunk to the awful condition sketched by Paul in the first chapter of Romans, and of which Seneca said that virtue was not only rare, but nowhere, and whose mephitic odors, even at this distance, appall and nauseate the student, Paul preached personal and social purity. The body of the believer was the temple of the Holy Spirit, and whosoever defiled it God would judge and destroy. Marriage was honorable, but adulterers and whoremongers God would judge.

We turn back to Jesus and we find that He taught precisely the same thing. There was adultery even in a glance of the eye. Monogamy was God's plan for humanity from the time of the creation of the man and the woman, and divorce, except upon one ground, was adultery. He told men, figuratively speaking, to pluck out their eye or cut off their hand, rather than indulge in sin which would cast them into hell.

The world to which Paul preached was a hard, pagan world. It is impossible for us, today, to imagine how strange the doctrine of brotherly love and forgiveness of injury sounded in the ears of the people of Antioch, and Athens, and Corinth, and Rome. Men not only did not forgive their enemies, but thought it weak and dishonorable to do so. Suspicion, revenge, hate, these were the principles of relationship between enemies. But Paul teaches the law of love, of forbearance and forgiveness. "Bless them which persecute you: bless and curse not." "Avenge not yourselves, but rather give place to wrath." "Be not overcome with evil, but overcome evil with good." "Being reviled, we bless; being persecuted, we suffer it." "Be ye kind one to another, tenderhearted, forgiving one another, even as God for Christ's sake hath forgiven you." "Forbearing one another and forgiving one another, if any man have a quarrel against any: even as Christ forgave you, so also do ye."

When we go back to the Gospels we find that Jesus had said the same thing. "Forgive us our debts as we forgive our debtors." "Love your enemies and bless them which curse you." Until seventy times seven men are to forgive their brothers. When the Roman soldiers, in obedience to their orders, nailed Him to the Cross, His only rejoinder and protest was, "Father forgive them, for they know not what they do."

The ethical teaching of Paul reaches its lovely climax in his great hymn to Christian love. I listen to him as he stands upon that mount of exaltation and inspiration and pours out his marvelous song: "Though I speak with the tongues of men and of angels, and have not love, I am become as sounding brass or a tinkling cymbal. And though I have the gift of prophecy and understand all mysteries and all knowledge; and though I have all faith, and have not love, I am nothing. Love suffereth long and is kind; love envieth not; love vaunteth not itself, is not puffed up—Beareth all things, believeth all things, hopeth all things, endureth all things. Love never faileth."

As I listen to that song I hear the music of another singer as He teaches the people on the side of Galilee's mountain, saying unto them, "Love your enemies and pray for them which despitefully use you and persecute you"; or, as He rises from His knees on the night in which He was betrayed, after He has washed the disciples' feet, and says to them, "I have given you an example, that ye should do as I have done unto you. A new commandment give I unto you, that ye love one another." The music of Paul's great hymn blends in perfect harmony with the song of Jesus, for it was inspired by the spirit of Jesus, and goes up like sweet incense to heaven's gate.

The Way of Salvation

We have left for the last that one doctrine of Paul's in which it is alleged he departs altogether from Jesus, and adds something completely foreign to the teaching of Jesus, that is, his idea of how Christ saves the sinner. The chief complaint against Paul is not what he taught about God, and the personal claims of Christ, or the Christian morality which he proclaimed, or his ideas as to the consummation of human history by Christ's coming again to judge the quick and the dead, but what he taught about the way in which Christ saves the sinner. Even among unbelievers there is not the least doubt as to what Paul taught on this subject. It is indelibly stamped upon every page of his epistles. All his theology was centered in the Cross. "God forbid that I should glory," he cried, "save in the cross of the Lord Jesus Christ." The motto of his whole ministry was what he wrote to the Christian disciples at Corinth, "I am determined to know nothing among you save Jesus Christ and Him crucified." That was the one great fact of his preaching. To this truth of the death of Christ for sin all else was ancillary and subsidiary; "for I delivered unto you *first of all* how that Christ died for our sins according to the Scriptures."

Unmistakable as is the place of preeminence which Paul gave to the death of Christ, his explanation of the meaning of that death is not less unmistakable. Christ died *for* our sins. He was made sin in our behalf. He was our substitute before the law of God. When the guilty and condemned sinner renounces all claim to self-righteousness and the favor of God, and confessing his sin, puts his faith in Christ as the One who has answered for him and satisfied the law of God in his behalf, then the sinner shares in the righteousness of Christ and being justified by faith is pardoned and accepted by God. By this method of dealing with man's sin, punishing it in the death of Christ, yet at the same time on the ground of that death forgiving it, God was both just and merciful. He remains just, yet the justifier of them that believe in Jesus.

The death of Christ thus is an exhibition of the punishment which sin deserves, and at the same time, of the marvelous love and grace of God, who commended His love to us in that while we were yet sinners Christ died for us. This is what we mean by Pauline theology. It is Paul's doctrine of the Cross. This is the theme which sets in full operation the splendid machinery of Paul's intellect and evokes in his heart wonder and praise at the depth of the riches of the redeeming love of God for sinners, especially when Paul remembers with pangs of contrition that he was the chief of sinners and once persecuted the Christ whom now he adores. When Paul said, "For me to live is Christ," he meant the Christ who bore his sin on the Cross and who by His substitution and expiation provided for his pardon and reconciliation. "I live," he says, "by the faith of the Son of God, who loved me and gave Himself for me."

But now we have those who say that while this is the teaching of Paul it is not the teaching of Jesus. Jesus, they say, taught forgiveness, but upon the ground of repentance, not upon the ground of His death upon the Cross. When the prodigal said, "Father, I have sinned," he was forgiven by the father. So God forgives the returning sinner. But Paul's doctrine of forgiveness is one based on the old Hebrew custom of sacrifice, the idea that a sacrifice must be made to God in order to propitiate Him and secure His favor and pardon. Thus, it is alleged, do Jesus and Paul differ completely about the fundamental truth of Christianity, the forgiveness of sin.

The only way in which we can find out whether Jesus differs from Paul as to the way of salvation is to see if this way of salvation taught by Paul is absent from, and not only absent from, but contrary to, the teachings of Jesus as they are recorded in the

Gospels. This will now be our task. Our examination brings to light the following facts.

1. *Jesus, like Paul, gives preeminent place to His death.* It is evident from the reading of the Four Gospels that their authors considered the death of Christ the preeminent fact of His ministry. Only two of the four evangelists tell of the birth of Christ; only two of the Temptation; only two of the Sermon on the Mount; only two tell of the Ascension. The Transfiguration, the Lord's Supper and the Agony in the Garden have no place in John's Gospel; the sketches of the Resurrection are brief. But all of the Gospels relate in full the betrayal, arrest, denial, trial, torture and death of Christ. "The fulfillment of type and shadow, of the hopes of patriarchs, of the expectations of prophets, yea, and of the dim longings of a whole lost and sinful world, must be declared by the whole evangelistic company; the four streams that go forth to water the earth must here meet in a common channel; the four winds of the Spirit of Life must here be united into one." This fact demands an explanation. Old Testament saints and prophets are dismissed in a few words. In the Gospels only a few lines are given to the death of John the Baptist, whom Jesus called the greatest man the world had ever seen. Luke, who gives so careful and lengthy an account of the death of Jesus, dismisses the Apostle James with a half-dozen words, when he was slain by Herod. Nor was it mere reverence for the person of Jesus, nor faith in the Resurrection, that made these men dwell so much on His death. It can only have been because that when they wrote they attached to His death the most profound significance. Where did they get that idea and impression? It must have been from Jesus Himself.

As a future fact the death of Christ was present with Him from the very beginning of His ministry. Jesus knew the meaning of John's allusion when he cried, "Behold the Lamb of God which taketh away the sin of the world." At the first passover He said, "Destroy this temple, and in three days I will raise it up," meaning the temple of His body. To Nicodemus, a few days afterward, He said that "as Moses lifted up the serpent in the wilderness, even so must the Son of Man be lifted up." When the Jews insisted upon a sign, He said that as Jonah was in the belly of the whale, even so the Son of Man should be three days and three nights in the heart of the earth. In His parable of the Good Shepherd, He referred to His approaching death, and again in His parable of how the husbandmen killed the heir and son. Most tenderly, too, when the disciples rebuked Mary for the costly gift of the ointment and pure nard which she had poured over His head and His feet, He said to let her alone, for she had kept it against the day of His burying. When the Greeks came to visit Him, in His moods of alternate jubilation and dread He cried out, "I, if I be lifted up, will draw all men unto me." On the mount of transfiguration He spoke with Moses and Elijah concerning His decease which He should accomplish at Jerusalem.

Nor were His references to His death just occasional or incidental, for three of the evangelists tell us that in the most direct and careful and positive way He taught the disciples both the fact and the manner of His death—that He would be betrayed into the hands of the Jewish rulers, who in turn would hand Him over to the Gentiles, that is, the Romans, who would put Him to death by crucifixion. For the beginning of this instruction Jesus chose one of the most impressive moments of His ministry, when Peter had publicly confessed Him as the Son of the Living God. Then it was that Jesus from that time forth began to show unto His disciples where and how He would be put to death. Matt. 16:21. "The Son of Man must suffer many things, and be rejected of the elders and chief priests and scribes, and be slain, and be raised the third day. Let these sayings sink down into your ears, for the Son of Man shall be delivered into the hands of men." Luke 9:22, 44. These sayings did "sink down" into their ears and into their hearts. That is why the death of Christ fills so large a space in the Gospels.

In addition to these frequent references to His death, whether incidental or deliberated, direct or veiled, and which in themselves must have impressed the disciples, there is the striking fact of the way in which Jesus felt towards His death. When the Greeks came to visit Him, and in them He saw the future conquests of the Cross, He cried out in joy; but the next moment, when He realized anew what the victory would cost, as He saw Himself the offering for sin, He cried out, "Now is My soul troubled, and what shall I say? Father, save Me from this hour!" Strange that the Victor should thus pray to be saved from the hour of victory!

At the Last Supper, when Jesus saw Judas sitting at the table and knew that in a few hours he would betray Him, and thus start Him on the path to the cross, John says that He was "troubled in spirit." For a little while He was able to throw off that deep agitation of the soul, when with all His sublime qualities of heart and mind at full command He breathed over the disciples His tender last farewell.

But in the Garden of Gethsemane it returned to trouble Him. He began to be sorrowful, and said to His disciples, Peter, James and John, "My soul is exceeding sorrowful, even unto death." Then, unable to endure even their intimacy, He withdrew from them about a stone's cast and entered into His agony and sweat as it were great drops of blood, and prayed, "O My Father, if it be possible, let this cup pass from me!" Jesus had passed under the cloud of suffering which was not to lift till the last great Cry on the Cross had been uttered. That suffering, either anticipated, or in the very hour of the crucifixion, must have been more than the natural shrinking of the body from pain. There is something deeper and more mysterious in it. It reached its climax when it wrung from Him the awful cry, "My God, my God, why hast thou forsaken me?" In view of what Jesus said before by way of explaining His death and what He and His disciples said afterwards, we believe that this strange agony and suffering was that of One whose soul was made an offering for sin; that in that death He was dying the sinner's condign death; and without such explanation that experience of Christ on the cross is one which may well fill us with dismay, for then it would tell us that as God forsook Christ, so He may forsake us. But so far our point is simply to demonstrate that the attitude of Jesus toward His death, both His frequent references to it and His anguish of soul as He contemplated it and encountered it, shows that even if He had said nothing at all as to the relation of His death to human sin and redemption, His death would stand out as the one great fact of His ministry, demanding some kind of an explanation, and making it perfectly reasonable that one of His followers, speaking of Him, should say, "For I delivered unto you, first of all, how that Christ died for our sins."

2. *Jesus gives the same meaning to His death that Paul does,* namely, that it is a substitutionary death for the sinner. We have seen

that the space in the four Gospels devoted to the death of Christ, the frequent and careful references of Jesus to it, and His strange and mysterious suffering in it, and in contemplation of it, give beyond all doubt a primary significance to His death. But what was that meaning? Why did He die? We know what the answer of Paul is, and the answer of historic Christianity, and even if Jesus had given no explanation of His death, the explanation of the letters of Paul would be the only reasonable explanation. But what did Jesus say? Did He give any explanation, and if so, is that explanation the same as that of Paul and historic Christianity? This is the issue.

Fortunately, Jesus was not silent. That He did not enter into an elaborated account of the relationship of His death to the sin of the world, such as we have in the letter of Paul to the Romans, for example, is not strange. In the first place, any explanation before His death must necessarily have differed, not in content, but in form, from the explanations which came after His death; and in the second place, the explanation of the Savior will be stated in a different way than the explanation of the sinner. Jesus' explanation is that of the Redeemer; Paul's explanation is that of the redeemed sinner. Jesus expected and made provision for an enlargement upon what He taught, and especially upon what He had taught on this very subject of His death, for He said, "I have yet many things to say unto you, but ye cannot bear them now. But when the Spirit of truth is come, He will guide you into all truth." Chrysostom, therefore, was not speaking in reckless enthusiasm of Paul, when he said he would like to see the dust of that mouth which lifted the truth on high and through which "Christ spake the great and secret things, and greater than in His own person." Christ did speak through Paul greater things than in His own person, that is, more fully, because men could then receive them. As Dr. Dale finely put it in his work on the Atonement, "The real truth is that while He came to preach the Gospel, His chief object in coming was that there might be a Gospel to preach."

But there is nothing that Paul said about the death of Christ which Jesus Himself did not utter in its preliminary form. In His address, recorded in John's Gospel, Jesus likened Himself to the shepherd of the flock, not at all in the way in which David, in the

Twenty-third Psalm, speaks of the shepherd and what he does for the flock, leading it into green pastures and beside the still waters, but as a shepherd who lays down his life for the flock. A shepherd might give up his life in defense of his flock in the struggle with robbers or with wild beasts; but Jesus makes it clear that He lays down His life voluntarily: "No man taketh it from me." This does not tell us that the death of Jesus is for the sins of men, but it does tell us that it was a unique death, and that it bore to men some relationship quite distinct from that of men who have died the most heroic and self-sacrificing death. In His conversation with Nicodemus, He not only tells him that a man must have a new life in God, be born again, but tells him how and at what a price that life may be secured— "For as Moses lifted up the serpent in the wilderness, even so must the Son of Man be lifted up, that whosoever believeth on him should not perish, but have everlasting life. For God so loved the world that he gave his only Son." There the death of Christ for the life of men is clearly taught.

Again, Jesus comes very close to the central thought of His death when He rebuked the disciples for their striving for place and taught them humility and service for others, saying, "For even the Son of Man came not to be ministered unto, but to minister, and to give his life a ransom for many." The word ransom needed no explanation in that day. Ransom was money paid for the return of a lost possession; it was the atonement money paid by every Jew to avert the judgments of God; it was the price paid to redeem a man from captivity and slavery; it was the price paid to save a man from death.

In any discussion on this subject it should be borne in mind that a very important part of the teaching of Jesus lies in the period of the forty days between the Resurrection and the Ascension. I think that much of the well-formulated Christian theology which we meet as soon as we enter the Book of the Acts was given to the disciples by Jesus during this period, and that together with the confirmation of the fact of His bodily Resurrection this purpose of doctrinal instruction was the reason for Christ's wait of forty days before He ascended into heaven.

The sermon preached to the two on the road to Emmaus shows us what was the content of the instruction of Jesus about the Kingdom of God, to which Luke refers in the first chapter of the

Acts. It was a message of redemption from sin through His death. In the sermon He preached to Cornelius, Peter gives a summary of Christian theology—Christ, the Fulfiller of prophecy, Christ, the Judge of the whole earth, and Christ, the Redeemer from sin. Peter says that this was the message given by Jesus to the disciples between the Resurrection and the Ascension. We may well suppose that these are but fragments of a rich and full redemptive teaching between the Resurrection and the Ascension of Christ.

There are many other passages which might be quoted, but the one great explanation which Christ gave us of His death is found in the celebration of the feast which was to commemorate that death. In order that there might be no misapprehension of His meaning, and that the purpose of His death might not be left to uncertain allusion or reference, or to be inferred from His anguish in Gethsemane, or His agony on the Cross, Jesus selected the night of His betrayal as the solemn hour for showing in the plainest and most unmistakable terms the meaning of the death He was to die on the morrow. Neither the taunts of His foes nor the requests of His friends drew from Him this great and beautiful explanation.

Language changes from age to age, and in transmitting thought from one generation to another there is always some risk of the true and original idea being lost sight of. It was wise forethought, therefore, on the part of Jesus to explain His death by a sacred rite, whose symbols and elements could speak a universal language. As they were eating the Passover supper, Jesus took bread and said, "Take, eat; this is my body which is broken for you; this do in remembrance of me." Then He took the cup and gave thanks and gave it to them, saying, "Drink ye all of it, for this is my blood of the new covenant which is shed for many for the remission of sins."

We have four accounts of the institution of this rite, now called the Lord's Supper, the three in the Gospels and Paul's. In no two of them do we have the words of Jesus in precisely the same form, yet in all of them the same fundamental idea is preserved, that His death was in some peculiar and unusual sense for others, or, as it is stated in Matthew's Gospel, for the remission of sins. That was the grand purpose of the death of Christ. Leave out of the reckoning all the rest of the New Testament, what Peter and John, and

Philip and Paul say about Christ's death being for the remission of sins, and let the Gospels stand alone, and still you have that glorious truth, the refuge of the past ages, the hope of generations to come, the believer's only stay, the theme of the redeemed in heaven, that Christ through His death saves us from our sins.

But when you take, in addition to the four Gospels, that great literature which came from the heart and mind of one who felt himself to be the chief of sinners, and knew that Christ had greatly saved him, and place it side by side with the four Gospels, and compare one with the other, you discover that just as the one great fact of Paul's Epistles is the death of Christ, stamped in crimson on every page, so in the Gospels the one great fact is the death of Christ. And further, when you take the explanation which Paul's Epistles give of the meaning of the death of Christ, that it was for the remission of our sins, that He was our sin-offering, that He was our substitute, that He took our place, and compare that explanation with what Jesus Himself says of His death, you find it to be the same.

Pilate wrote over Him on the Cross the motto, "Jesus of Nazareth, the King of the Jews." But the real motto over the Cross was that of Jesus Himself, "This is my blood which is shed for many for the remission of sins." To that motto the answer of Paul, as he stands at the foot of the Cross, gazing at the Crucified, and the answer of all the generations of believers, and the rapturous song of the redeemed in heaven, was, is, and ever shall be, "The Son of God, who loved me and gave himself for me."

11

WILL ANOTHER JESUS DO?

If he that cometh preacheth another Jesus (2 Cor. 11:4).

In one of his letters to Christian believers in a city where he had preached, St. Paul speaks of the possibility of men coming to them who will preach "another Jesus." They would speak, of course, of the same historical person, but their conception of Him would be so different that it would be as if they were telling of an altogether different Jesus.

Another Jesus! It is a far cry from the Judaisers of Corinth and Galatia who would have made Christianity a religion of rites and customs and works, instead of a religion of redemption from sin, to the modernists who preach in many of our pulpits, today, and write in many of our magazines and have much to say about Jesus. But the Judaisers of the first century and the Modernists of the twentieth century are alike in this respect: they both present to the world "another Jesus." Great changes in the religious life and habits of a people come slowly and almost imperceptibly; there is no paroxysm to mark the transition from one form of faith to another. For this reason the astounding change which has come over the Protestant conception of Christianity is only partially realized, and in many quarters not at all. Ecclesiastical boards and agencies go calmly on planning their progressive work and using the language of the Protestantism of yesterday as if it expressed the belief of the Protestantism of today, whereas the fact is that so great has been the change which has come over the Protestant Churches that it is no exaggeration to say that, in some places, Protestantism is offering to the world, today, "another Jesus." This statement, I know, will be warmly resented in many quarters, and by none more warmly than by those who have gone the farthest in proclaiming "another Jesus."

The Roman Catholic Church is more awake to this stupendous change which has been going on in the Protestant Church than those within the pale of the Reformation Churches. A writer in a recent number of a Catholic journal thus sums up the situation in the Protestant Church as viewed by a Catholic:

"The changed attitude of Protestantism towards the Bible is nothing short of a complete right about face. For the Reformers there was no other rule of faith. In the inspired Word of God was the only truth clearly spoken to men, obviously intelligible, patent to all who ran or read. Now professors in Protestant seminaries throw out, with a careless toss of the hand, whole books of the Scripture, essential passages in the Gospels, any chapter or verse that does not please their fancy. As for faith without works, we have seen that original doctrine of Protestantism stood on its head, until it reads now, not faith without works, but works without faith; or, to put it more plainly, it makes no difference what you believe, as long as you do what you consider right. No wonder that Protestantism has become year by year less religious and more purely social in character. The day is past when Protestantism thinks its faith worth fighting for."

The indictment is severe; yet many earnest souls in the Protestant Communion confess that there is much in the Protestant Church which affords a basis for it. Read the books of sermons, talk with the average Protestant layman, sit in the churches on the Sabbath and listen to the sermons, and you will realize that in many Protestant circles the great question, "What shall I do to be saved?" and the great answer which created the Protestant Church, "Salvation is of faith," are no longer spoken. The Protestant mind no longer seems to trouble itself with that greatest of all problems. The excuse given is that it has something infinitely more important to attend to, that is, the salvation of the social order. Hence the terrible paralysis, and blight, and weariness, that have come over Protestant worship.

The Protestant Churches were established in the beginning to answer in some way, and with some particular emphasis, that question as to the salvation of a soul. All the creeds, and all the hymns, and all the sacraments, take for granted that that is the main issue. But now, upon this creedal, confessional, individualistic branch of religion there has been a vast effort to graft a secularistic conception of Christianity. But the grafting has not been a success. The native stock has been hurt and wounded, so much so that it can give neither the fruit nor shade for the soul of man which once it did, and the new branch, the scion, is already dead, although the shaking of the branch by the vagrant winds and the rustling of its withered leaves make a considerable noise, and to a passer-by, who did not look too closely, might give the impression of vitality and enterprise.

Volumes might be written to explain how and why this change has taken place. But the piercing phrase of Paul tells us all in two words, "Another Jesus." Who can doubt that such a Jesus is now being proclaimed? In two respects the Jesus of Modernism, that is, the Jesus of many of the Protestant pulpits, and many of the Protestant colleges and seminaries, is "another" Jesus than that of the New Testament. First, important facts are missing from the story of His life; and secondly, the facts which remain are so reinterpreted that what they present to us is another gospel and another Christ.

Let us commence with some of the facts in the life of our Lord which are not found in the life of this new Jesus. Every man's personality is made up of a certain number of facts, such as his parentage, the time and place of his birth, his education, his occupation, his home and family. It is not otherwise with the personality of our Lord, so far as His life upon earth is concerned. The initial fact of His earthly life was the fact of His birth. The Gospels not only tell us of the Incarnation of God in Jesus, but they tell us the manner of the Incarnation, that the Eternal Son of God became man by taking to Himself a true body and a reasonable soul, being conceived by the power of the Holy Spirit in the womb of the Virgin Mary, and born of her, yet without sin. Theories, interpretations, do not enter into this question, for it is a matter of fact. The Jesus of the New Testament was born of the Virgin Mary.

But it is precisely at this initial and fundamental fact in the life of

Jesus that the Jesus of Modernism begins to draw away from the Jesus of the Gospels. The Jesus of Modernism was not born of the Virgin Mary. The New Testament statements to that effect are to be understood as the pious efforts of earnest men to account for the evident preeminence of the Person of Jesus. They fell back on the old pagan idea of miraculous conception, and phrased their idea of the birth of Jesus in what a prominent present-day preacher describes as a "biological miracle which the modern mind cannot receive." Just why the "modern mind" should be exempted from this part of Christian faith is not clear, for we remember that Cerinthus, a contemporary of St. John, found the Virgin Birth a biological miracle which his ancient mind could not receive. Some Modernists who reject the initial fact of the New Testament life of Jesus warmly asseverate their faith in Jesus as God and as their Redeemer. I ask them where they get their knowledge of this Jesus who is God's Son and the world's Redeemer? They tell me from the New Testament, not seeming to understand that by rejecting the Virgin Birth as unhistorical, they have confessed that the entire narrative is untrustworthy, for if the initial fact recorded is false, why should we take seriously the other facts?

But, says the Modernist, "Why insist upon a Virgin Birth?" Could not the Son of God have become incarnate in Jesus through the process of ordinary generation, with Joseph for His father, and Mary for His mother? To be sure God who is almighty, could have done so, although had that been the method of the Incarnation it would be a mystery a thousand times more perplexing than what we have.

In a recently published sermon, a Presbyterian minister who objects to the declaration of the 1923 General Assembly that the Virgin Birth is an essential doctrine of the Scriptures and of the Presbyterian standards, appeals to an utterance of Dr. Francis L. Patton, the former President of Princeton University and of Princeton Theological Seminary. According to his oft-quoted utterance, Dr. Patton said we have no reason to believe that God could not have incarnated Himself through a human father as well as through a human mother. In the sense in which Dr. Patton must have said this, no one would take exception to it. It is true that we have no reason to think that Almighty God could not have incarnated Himself through a human father as well as through a human mother. It is also true that we have no reason to think that He did.

But it is not a question at all of what is possible with God. God might have had an altogether different race. He might have chosen some other plan of redemption. It is not a question of what God can do, or might have done, but what God has done. In the narrative of the Virgin Birth the Gospels tell us how the Word became flesh. If, therefore, a man comes to me preaching a Jesus who was not born of the Virgin Mary, it is another Jesus than that of the New Testament.

With the great miracle of His Incarnation thus rejected, it is not strange that we should very quickly discover that the Jesus of the Modernist is a Jesus who Himself did no miracles. The ground upon which the miracles are rejected cannot be the lack of evidence, for the evidence for the miracles is just the same as that for any of the facts of the life of Jesus. The evidence that Jesus stilled the tempest is just the same as it is for His being asleep on a pillow in the stern of the boat. The evidence for His walking *upon* the sea is just the same as the evidence for His walking *by* the sea and calling His disciples.

The real ground of rejection is a repugnance for the supernatural as related to Christianity. The Modernist is in reality a disciple of Hume, whose position was that miracles do not happen, therefore they never happened. Instead of rejecting miracles on the ground of lack of evidence, the Modernist ignores the evidence altogether. The new knowledge of the operation of the laws of nature which man has acquired is put forward as exempting the modern mind from any serious consideration of the miracles. But when this reason is given we wonder why so much emphasis is laid upon the modern mind, for going through the pages of Origen's refutation of the assault of Celsus on Christianity, A.D. 161-180, we discover that the second century mind of Celsus, unschooled in modern science, was just as unwilling and unable to accept a miracle as the mind of the most vocal Modernist of our own day. If many crimes have been committed in the name of religion, it is likewise true that many rejections of the Christian revelation which are born of fallen man's natural enmity to God, and have nothing whatever to do with science, have been disguised in the garments of some discovery or hypothesis of science.

However, the real issue is not what the modern mind can or

cannot accept, but, did Jesus work miracles? The Gospels say He did work as many as thirty-three miracles. The Modernist, on the other hand, gives us a Jesus who, like John the Baptist, "did no miracles." But a Jesus from whose history the miracles are deleted is no Jesus at all. The miraculous is so woven into the fabric of the garment of our Lord's life that you cannot tear it out without destroying the garment itself, for even if we take out of the Gospels the records of the works of Jesus, we are still confronted by a Jesus who, in His teaching, referred to His power to work miracles and in the most uncompromising manner claimed that He worked miracles. A Modernist preacher tells me he cannot "swallow" that story of Jesus walking on the sea. Very well. But what is he going to do with the Jesus, who, when asked by the messengers of John in prison, "Art thou he that should come, or look we for another?" answered, "Go and tell John that the lame walk, the deaf hear, the blind see, the lepers are cleansed, the dead are raised up and the poor have the gospel preached unto them"? Even with the recorded miracles deleted, the Gospels still present to us a Jesus who claimed that He worked miracles.

It is not that we hanker after a prodigy, but that we long for Christ. It is not a miracle that we want, but Christ, and the only Christ we can have is the Christ who worked miracles. This Jesus of the Modernist who did no miracles may be a very wonderful person, a great teacher, example, dreamer, reformer, and so on. The only trouble with him is that he never existed. The only Jesus who existed was a Jesus who worked miracles. I prefer the Jesus who worked miracles and who existed, to the Jesus who did no miracles and who never existed.

But let us turn now to a great fact in the life of Jesus which the Modernist tells us he has no desire to delete from the Gospels, the death of Jesus on the Cross. In the New Testament, and even in the anticipatory statements of Jesus Himself, such as, "This cup is the new covenant in my blood, which is shed for many, for the remission of sins," the place and the meaning of the death of Jesus is so plain that the wayfaring man though a fool need not err therein. Paul tells us that he delivered unto his converts "first of all," as the primal truth, to which all else was subsidiary and ancillary, that Christ died for our sins according to the Scriptures, that is, in fulfillment of prophecy. Both John and Paul give us clear definitions of God as love, and they both agree in saying that the grand exhibition of the love of God for mankind was the death of Christ. It was a substitutionary and sacrificial death, Jesus taking the sinner's sins and the sinner's curse, and by His suffering and His perfect obedience making possible the forgiveness of the sinner. No better short statement of the meaning of the death of Christ can be found than that of Burns in *The Cotter's Saturday Night*, where he describes the patriarchal father reading at family worship from the Christian volume—

> How guiltless blood for guilty man was shed.

But that is not what the Modernist means by the death of Christ. He says he believes in vicarious suffering, that on the Cross, Christ suffered for others, in harmony with the law which runs through the whole creation, the strong suffering for the weak and the weak for the strong, and the good for the bad, and the mother for the child, and the past for the present. But that Christ in His suffering bore the sinner's penalty and made satisfaction for the broken law, or that Christ's death had any effect upon God—that, the Modernist cannot accept. He gets very angry about it, and of all the ideas of historic Christianity it is this basilar idea of the atonement, Christ's death FOR sin and FOR sinners, which stirs his modern mind to righteous indignation. He says such a thing is both impossible and immoral; impossible and inadequate, because every man must bear his own transgression, and nothing done by another man can help him; immoral, because it is the innocent man who suffers and is punished instead of the guilty. As a prominent minister of the Presbyterian Church said to an anxious parishioner who wanted to know why he never preached on the Atonement, "I certainly would not ask my son to die for the sins of someone else, and I do not believe God would have done that."

When asked to tell just what he does mean by the death of Jesus on the Cross, the Modernist, if you can persuade him to emerge for a little from the "low visibility" where he hides himself in his rhetoric, will confess that all the death of Christ means to him is that it was the great example of perfect obedience and perfect love for others, and as such, must have a profound effect upon the moral nature of every man who contemplates it. Thus what Paul called the "offence of the Cross" has ceased. The idea in the Cross which offends the mind of man, whether it be the modern, the mediaeval, or the ancient mind, is the idea of condemnation, of sin, of guilt, of substitution and mediation. The Cross of the New Testament is a Cross in which a man either glories as Paul did, or a Cross which he hates and despises and at whose victim his unregenerate nature cries out as did the railers at the Crucifixion, "Come down from the Cross!" This sweet, altruistic, vicarious Cross of the Modernist Christian, what has that to do with the Cross of Calvary, the Cross of expiation and atonement? And this new Jesus whose death is the perfect example, exerting such a profound influence upon men's moral nature, who is he? Whoever he is, he certainly is not the Jesus of the New Testament, the Jesus who was delivered for our sins and rose again for our justification, and by whose blood, being cleansed and justified, we have peace with God the Father.

It is a sad task, this study of the preaching of "another Jesus" in Protestant circles today. But the encouraging, the reassuring, thing is that in every Protestant Church there is the sound of commotion. Believing men are at length awakening to the fact that the new Jesus who is being preached is *not* the Jesus of the New Testament. They are awakening to the fact that this "other Jesus" has nothing in common with Jesus of Nazareth, declared to be the Son of God with power by the resurrection from the dead; and what is more to the point, they are awakening to a realization that this other Jesus of the Modernists is not a Jesus who can save and deliver.

A damaged Christ can do nothing for a damaged soul or a damaged world. In all the Protestant Churches there is a body of men who love their ecclesiastical house and home, and would go out from it with sorrow and pain of heart. They will do all that they can to contend against the invasion of Modernism with its pseudo-Jesus who can neither save nor condemn. But should it become apparent that the Churches, as at present established, are going to depart from the faith of the New Testament and preach "another Jesus" and this other gospel, "which is not another," then they who still believe in the Jesus of the New Testament will not hesitate for a moment. They will rend the unity of their respective Churches and go out from among them and join in a Christian fellowship where Jesus is King of Kings and Lord of Lords. From the river unto the ends of the earth this company of believers are marshaling their forces and stretching out eager hands of faith and communion to their brethren in all the Churches. These men know in whom they have believed. They know what their faith is, and stand ready to state it and to defend it, if need be, to suffer and die for it. To all those who openly attack Christianity to destroy it, and to all those who, under various disguises, seek to substitute "another Jesus" for the Christ of the centuries, their answer is the magnificent defiance of F. W. H. Meyer's *St. Paul,*

> Whoso hath felt the spirit of the Highest
> Cannot confound Him, or doubt Him or deny.
> Yea, though with one voice, O world, thou deniest,
> Stand thou on that side, for on this am I.

12

Have New Foes Risen Against Christ?

Is there a new thing whereof it may be said, See, this is new? It hath been long ago in the ages which were before us (Eccles. 1:10).

There is nothing new under the sun, especially, in the way of unbelief. Of late there has been no little stir in all our churches because of the expression of certain opinions about the Bible and the Christian faith. The newspapers are supposed to give their readers what is new, and the prominent place which the reports of these opinions about Christ and the Bible occupy in the newspapers may have a tendency to create the impression in the minds of the people that there really is something new about these views, and that the Christian Church is confronted by a new kind of enemy, armed with a new and most dangerous weapon. But if the ground of the alarm felt by earnest Christians in our churches is that either new facts or new opinions are now being used to break down faith, they may relieve their minds of all anxiety. The words of the wise man apply with particular appositeness to what is popularly spoken of as "new" theology and "modernism": In all of it, "is there a new thing whereof it may be said, See, this is new? It has been long ago in the ages which were before us."

The metempsychosis of error and heresy is a very curious thing. When the error or false teaching has been dead for generations, so long that the volumes which entombed it are worm-eaten and the fierce controversies which raged about it are deep in oblivion, lo, the thing comes to life again! The ugly chrysalis of unbelief is transformed into a brilliant butterfly, after which the would-be doubters of the day go in hot and eager pursuit. By-and-by they grow weary in their pursuit, and the butterfly itself loses its vitality as the brilliant colors fade from its wings and it sinks back into the earth whence it came. The new theologies and the new conceptions of Christianity are new only to the age which is beguiled into listening to them and following after them. The history of Christianity shows that in successive generations they have been looked upon as new, whereas they are as old as human unbelief, and that is as ancient as man.

Almost the first sentence of the Bible is, "God said," and almost the first sentence of temptation in the Bible is, "*Hath* God said?" The great question of religion is, whether or not God has spoken to man, and whether or not we have a true record of that revelation. Has He, Whom dimly we take to be our Creator and our God, come out from the darkness and the silence, and spoken a word to man? The destiny of a race hangs upon the answer to that question. Christianity presents itself to humanity as God's word, His speech, His revelation, for the good of man. "And God said," is the chord struck so magnificently at the beginning of the book. It follows us with its deep reverberations wherever we go in this many-chambered palace of the Bible and of Christian faith. "And God said," "Hear ye the Word of the Lord!" "Thus saith the Lord!"

Yet, at the very beginning came the Tempter with his sly insinuation, "Yea, and hath God said?" This first sentence of unbelief will be the last also, for to create doubt as to whether or not God has spoken, is the only way in which the powers of darkness can persuade the soul to rebel against God and refuse the great salvation which He has provided. All forms of unbelief, ancient, medieval and modem, are in substance but a repetition of that first question put to the woman by the Tempter. God has never said anything to a fallen race which was not immediately questioned, denied, ridiculed. For every, "Thus saith the Lord!" there has been an answering, "Hath God said?" The attack on the Bible, on God's Word, on revealed religion, is as old as man's mind. Should anyone say to us, then, concerning some reported attack upon Christianity, "See, this is new!" remember it was the same long ago in the ages which were before us. The same enemies have launched their fiery darts against the Church and the Bible. The mind that invented them was just as keen, and the arm which hurled them was just as strong, as are the mind and the arm which devise them and hurl them today. Yet the Church and the Bible remain.

The Virgin Birth

This general proposition I wish to develop and illustrate by a comparative study of what men in different ages have said against Christ and His Church. We might start with a doctrine of Christianity which is much under discussion today, the Virgin Birth of our Lord. One of the most popular preachers in England, in a series of sermons on the Apostles' Creed, says of the Virgin Birth, "The historical evidence is not conclusive either way. It leads, and must lead, to a verdict of not proven. . . . I think it (the doctrine of the Virgin Birth) found its place in the Creed, and has kept it, because the purity of Jesus seemed to His followers to demand such a miracle—a unique personality demanded a unique birth." According to this statement, it was the effort to account for the "unique personality of Jesus" that led to the invention of the story of the Virgin Birth and its inclusion in the Creed.

Side by side with these utterances from Christian pulpits let me place a paragraph from Thomas Paine's *Age of Reason*: "It is, however, not difficult to account for the credit that was given to the story of Jesus Christ being the Son of God. He was born when the heathen mythology had still some fashion in the world, and that mythology had prepared the people for the belief of such a story. Almost all the extraordinary men that lived under the heathen mythology were reputed to be the sons of some of their gods. It was not a new thing at that time to believe a man to have been celestially begotten."

Going back to the second century, we find in the True Discourse of Celsus, the great assailant of Christianity in his days, a similar rejection of the Virgin Birth. What Celsus said is preserved in the refutation of it found in the works of Origen I, chapters 28-37. The Jew whom Celsus introduces to confute Jesus, charges Him with having invented the story of His birth from a Virgin, and upbraids Him with having been born of a poor spinning woman who had been turned out of doors by her husband, a carpenter by trade, because she was guilty of adultery with a soldier named Panthera. Celsus also seeks to discredit the Virgin Birth by likening it to the tales of Greek fables about the Danae, and Melanippe, and Auge, and Antiope. His special contribution to the literature of the Virgin Birth is found in his preservation of the Jewish story of a Roman soldier, Panthera. He boldly and shamelessly filled in the gap created by denying the Virgin Birth, by supplying a supposed father. This is logical, but more than the Modernists of today will dare.

Going still further back, to the first century, we come to Cerinthus, a contemporary of St. John, who held the Virgin Birth to be impossible, and made Jesus the son of Joseph and Mary, and who received divine powers at the baptism. When, therefore, one refers to the Virgin Birth as a "biological miracle which the modern mind cannot receive," he is telling us nothing new, either about the rejection of the Gospel narratives or the mind of man, for the eighteenth century mind of Thomas Paine found it just as difficult to receive; and Celsus and Cerinthus, one in the second and the other in the first century of the Christian era, were just as much opposed to the idea of the Virgin Birth as our Modernists of today. The Modernists are simply saying what the unbelievers of every age have said. The only difference is that Celsus and Paine said it from outside the Church, whereas the Modernist says it from inside the Church.

THE ATONEMENT

The Christian Church has never ignored the Cross of Christ. How He died for our sins, according to the Scriptures, was the truth that Paul and the other apostles delivered, *first of all*, to the people to whom they preached. The great presupposition of Christianity is, that man is a sinner, and that Christianity is God's great remedy for sin; that God was in Christ reconciling the world to Himself, not man reconciling himself to God, but God, and that God did this through the eternal sacrifice of Christ on the Cross, "for it was the good pleasure of the Father, through Him, to reconcile all things unto Himself, having made peace through the blood of His Cross, through Him, I say, whether things upon the earth or things in the heavens." The grand stream of Christian life and history has never deviated from its true course which takes it ever close to the Cross, as some western river flows close to the great rock which rises from its banks. As a Church, the Christian Church has proclaimed Christ and Him crucified; there it has grounded all its truth and rested all its radiant hopes.

Yet, from age to age, we have had within and without the Church teachings and utterances which would take the meaning and the power out of the Cross, so that its "offence" has ceased, that is, the idea that on the Cross Christ took the sinner's place. Of late there have been frequent and bitter outbreaks against the Cross as Paul preached it and gloried in it. I shall quote some of these utterances.

Caricature perhaps brings out the true features as well as an ordinary portrait. In a recent sermon a well-known preacher describes what he calls a special theory of the Atonement as held by "Evangelicals," "that the blood of our Lord, shed in substitutionary death, placates an alienated Deity and makes possible welcome for the returning sinner." In a published letter he says of the Atonement, "There never has been any redemption from sin and degradation except through vicarious sacrifice. . . . What I do believe is that Jesus Christ is the Divine Love taking on Himself the sins of the world that He might save us. I not only believe this, but I see no difficulty in believing it. What I do not believe is a theory of the Atonement which is founded, not upon this universal fact of vicarious atonement, but upon a governmental theory of substitutionary punishment which was outlawed from every decent penal system on earth long ago."

A much more shocking utterance will be found in a book by a professor in a theological seminary:

"Paul's idea of law, of penalty, of expiation, offends the modern sense of justice and contradicts our ethical values at every point of contact. Without caricature it may be compared to ideas that prevail in certain police circles today. A sensational crime is committed; the public is greatly roused and demands detection and punishment of the criminal. This the police are unable to accomplish, but obviously something must be done to silence public clamor; so they 'frame up' a case against someone who can plausibly be made the scapegoat. He is convicted by perjury, the public cry is silenced, the majesty of the law has been vindicated, justice is satisfied! But we are no longer content with that brand of justice. We insist that the guilt of the guilty cannot be expiated, justice cannot be satisfied, by the punishment of the innocent. Yet our own theology teaches and continues to teach us that the Almighty could find no better expedient to save men than to 'frame up' a case against His own Son, and put to death the innocent for the guilty. And that which fills us with horror when done by man to man, we praise and glorify when done by God to God."

In another book, *I Believe*, a popular English preacher imagines a man who has been asked to come and be saved on the ground of Christ's bitter suffering, answering: "What I want to know is, Why did Jesus suffer? What good did His sufferings do? What good purpose was served by them which could not have been served without? If you cannot give me intelligible answers of some sort, I am prepared to pity Jesus, as I am prepared to pity any other noble visionary who has been put to death, because he was before his time, but I do not see why I should worship Him because of His sufferings, which are just one more gruesome act in this world's sordid tragedy of errors. I cannot see what good the sufferings of Jesus did, or why, if there be an Almighty God of Love, I could not have been saved without them. I cannot see why men should not have been forgiven, if they repented, without this brutal murder as a sacrifice. Jesus forgave men freely when He was on earth, and never Himself mentioned any other condition of forgiveness but repentance. Yet you say that a callous murder had to be committed before it was possible for God to forgive a repentant man. To be quite frank, this doctrine strikes me as being not merely incredible, but immoral as well."

This indictment of the doctrine of the Cross from the "man on the street"—but who, as a matter of fact, is far more ready to take the doctrine of the Cross, than some scholars and preachers who put into the mouth of the "man on the street" their own doubts—the author answers by saying that "plain men do not understand the justice that demands eternal punishment, and cannot picture a Father who requires propitiation before He forgives a repentant child." "The fact is our preachers spend their time explaining, not the Gospel, but the symbols and metaphors which its first evangelists used in the struggle to give its message to the men of their day, men whose minds moved in a different world from ours, whose religion was steeped in bloody sacrifices, whose states were ruled by despots, and whose idea of justice was full of cruelty and destitute of love. We sacrifice reason and imperil morality in order to keep these pseudo-sacred symbols and metaphors intact."

He then goes on to improve on the explanations of John and Peter and Paul, with their minds "steeped in bloody sacrifices," but who admittedly had some close contact with the Son of God, by telling us that it is Christ who saves and not the Cross; that the Cross was the most natural and inevitable thing in the world, "as natural and inevitable as all the rest of the hideous process by which life has been, and is being, evolved. We are saved not by what Christ was or did, but by what He is. The Cross is common; it is Christ who is unique." Having rejected the plain Scriptural explanation of the Cross, men are hard put to give any explanation, save to say, generally, that it tells us of the love of God. But the great act of God's love is left without any explanation.

In another book, *Modernism in Religion*,[1] the author refers thus to the old view of the Cross as a sacrifice: "The modernistic conception of salvation and how it is effected has little in common with theological theories. . . . So far as we have the spirit of Jesus, the spirit of self-sacrifice, just so far are we saved. . . . God needs no reconciling offering from man. Why not let the old theories go? Why not take Jesus' parable of the Prodigal Son as the simple and sufficient 'plan of salvation'? The blush of shame on the face of the self-banished returning son, and the Father's yearning heart going forth to welcome him! That is all."

So much for modern present-day statements about the death of Christ. Now let us trace that stream of denial back through the ages. First we go back a century, and in the lectures of the brilliant agnostic, Robert Ingersoll, we find this saying about the Atonement:

"The Christian system is, that if you will believe something, you can get credit for something that somebody else did; and as you are charged with the sin of Adam, you are credited with the virtues of the Lord."

1. *Modernism in Religion*, J. M. Sterrett.

Of the same tone is Paine's comment on the Atonement in *The Age of Reason:* "The Christian mythologists tell us that Christ died for the sins of the world, and that He came on purpose to die. That Christ's death does not prevent our dying is evident, because we all die; and with respect to the second explanation, including with it the natural death or damnation of all mankind, it is impertinently representing the Creator as coming off, or revoking sentence, by a pun or quibble upon the word death. That manufacturer of quibbles, St. Paul, has helped this quibble on, by making another quibble upon the word Adam. He makes there to be two Adams; *the one who sins in fact, and suffers by proxy; the other who sins by proxy, and suffers in fact.*"

Leaving Ingersoll and Paine, we take a long journey back to the father of them all, Celsus. Celsus' chief objection to Christianity seems to be that it offered forgiveness to sinners, to the vilest of the earth, in contrast with the mysteries which invited only the good and the pure to come to their celebrations. But in rejecting the sacrifice of Christ for sin, Celsus is more logical than the modernists. The modernists reject the sacrificial death for sin but still praise that death and dwell upon the incidents of our Lord's passion. But Celsus is more logical when he scoffs at our Lord's suffering, saying that He received no assistance from His Father and was unable to aid Himself, and reproaches Him with lack of fortitude in pain and suffering, saying that when the vinegar and the gall was offered Him to ease His pains "he rushed with open mouth to drink of them, and could not endure His thirst as any ordinary man frequently endures it"; that He weakly prayed to let the cup pass from Him in Gethsemane, and that there was nothing in His conduct to compare with the fortitude of Epictetus who, when his master was twisting his leg, said, "You will break my leg"; and when he had broken it said, "Did I not tell you that you would break it?

And there Celsus unwittingly laid his finger upon the one distinctive thing about the sufferings of Christ, the thing which he could not or would not understand, namely, that Christ was suffering for sin, and bearing the curse of sin. The Modernist wants to do away with the sacrificial death for sin, but still keep the pathetic figure of Gethsemane's shadows and the solitary sufferer of Golgotha. But Celsus was more logical than the Modernist, for

Christ in the midst of His trials presents a strange figure compared with Epictetus, or Socrates, or many a nameless man who has gone to the stake or the gibbet, *unless He is suffering for sin*, drinking the cup of human woe. If God is visiting upon Him the iniquities of us all, making Him to be sin who knew no sin, then we understand the prayer of Gethsemane, "O my Father, if it be possible, let this cup pass from me!" and the cry of Calvary, " My God, why hast thou forsaken me!"

The reason adduced by the so-called "Modernists" for rejecting the substitutionary atonement is that man has so developed morally that such an idea is repugnant to him. Just as in the case of miracles it is claimed that the progress and revelation of scientific research have made it impossible for the modern mind to accept a miracle like the Virgin Birth, or Christ walking on the sea, so with regard to the Atonement, they claim that the progress of human thought, the humanization of society, make it impossible to accept the New Testament doctrine of the Atonement. But just as in the case of miracles, we saw that the medieval and ancient mind, wholly uninstructed and unenlightened in modern science, found a miracle just as objectionable as the modern mind, so in the case of the Atonement the objections come not only from men of this modern day, the heir of the ages, the ripe product of the softening and refining influences of Christianity, but also from the mind of the doubter of the second century.

What makes the Atonement repugnant to the Modernists of today, to the agnostics of half a century ago, to the deists of the eighteenth century, to the unbelievers of the second century, to the Jews, to whom it was a stumbling block, and to the Greeks, to whom it was foolishness, is not any extraordinarily developed sense of justice, or true zeal for the righteousness of God, how the judge of all the earth must do that which is right, but a native objection to and repugnance for the implication of the Cross, namely, that we are sinners who for ourselves can do nothing; "for I thus judge that if Christ died for all, then had all died." This is the "offense" of the Cross, that it not only saves but condemns; that it takes all man's learning, strength, pride, fame, wealth, natural expectations, past achievements, and says, "This is nothing!"

That it is what the Cross says about sin that constitutes its chief offense to the human mind, is apparent by what Paine says of the

Christian teaching that man is a sinner: "It is by his being taught to contemplate himself as an outlaw, as an outcast, as a beggar, as a pauper, as one thrown as it were on a dunghill at an immense distance from his Creator, and who must make his approaches by creeping, and cringing to intermediate beings, that he conceives either a contemptuous disregard for everything under the name of religion, or becomes indifferent, or turns devout, what he calls devout. In the latter case, he consumes his life in grief, or the affectation of it." And in the same vein Celsus, who is always able to go the Modernist and the agnostic one better. He compares the Christians "to a flight of bats, or to a swarm of ants issuing out of their nests, or to frogs holding council in a marsh, or to worms crawling together in the corner of a dunghill and quarreling with one another as to which of them were the greatest sinners."

The Antiquity of Modernism

There is nothing peculiar about the expressions of disbelief in Christian doctrine which we hear on every side today. They are but echoes of the spirit of unbelief that is in the world from the beginning. It is not a question of the modern mind or the medieval mind, but the natural heart and mind of man which is enmity with God, and alienated from God. Christianity presents itself to men as a remedy for sin. But man, ancient, mediaeval, or modern, has never liked to confess that he is a sinner. Hence he has either openly rejected Christianity, or what is more common, and today most prevalent, he has tried to restate it and reinterpret its great doctrines so that they shall apply to this imaginary being who is not a lost sinner. But the attempt breaks down. Christianity is a religion intended for sinners and cannot be made to fit any other kind of man. The present chaotic condition of Christianity, so far as its beliefs are concerned, is due entirely to the fact that the great presupposition of Christianity, that man is a lost sinner who can do nothing for himself, and must perish unless Christ comes to save him, is either bitterly denied or coolly ignored.

We may talk as we will about the "new knowledge," the "progress of science," "progressive revelation," the "new world" we live in, the "static" rather than the "dynamic" idea of faith, and so on through all the catalogue of the favorite terms of Modernist theology; but that is not the cause or the origin of the neo-Christianity "another gospel which is not another," which is being preached in so many of our churches today. The real cause and source of it is man's unwillingness to take God's remedy for sin. Whether that unwillingness and that rejection of God's redemptive love be phrased in the terms of Celsus, or Volney, or Paine, or Ingersoll, or in the honied accents of Modernist teachers and preachers, it is at the bottom one and the same thing.

No man can become a Christian without the act of faith, and that act of faith, that taking Christ as Lord and Savior, presupposes taking one's self as a sinner. That men should refuse to do this is nothing new under the sun. Men today, as well as the men of yesterday, have that solemn, that awful liberty, the liberty to reject the Son of God. We plead with them not to do so. We call upon them to repent and believe on the Lord Jesus Christ and be saved. But if they will not believe, let them say so like men, and face the wrath of Him whose dying love they contemn. What we cannot tolerate in them is that they should array their unbelief in modern garments and try to persuade men that it is in any respect different from the unbelief which greeted the Son of God when He first came to save sinners, and which will continue to fight against Him until He has put all enemies under His feet.

When "Herod was dead, an angel of the Lord appeared in a dream to Joseph in Egypt, saying, Arise, and take the young child and his mother, and go into the land of Israel, for they are dead that sought the young child's life." Each new age has its successors to Herod who seek "the young child's life." Their purpose is the same from age to age, although new uniforms appear and new phrases are coined and new weapons are employed. But ever the contest comes to an end with the verdict of the Angel of the Lord, "They are dead that sought the young child's life." The generations of unbelief come and go, but the Eternal Child abides forever.

QUESTIONS FOR DISCUSSION

CHAPTER 1

1. On pages 9 and 10 of the attack on the doctrine of the Virgin Birth Macartney says: "Many declare that the credibility and significance of Christianity are in no way affected by the doctrine of the Virgin Birth, and some go so far as to say that the doctrine is a stumbling block to the faith . . . and that narratives of the Virgin Birth . . . arose in much the same way as the old legends and myths about the supernatural births of famous personages of the pagan world." Do you agree?
2. How do Macartney's comments about the great mystery of "the beginning of all life" relate to the modern anti-abortion, right-to-life movement?
3. Macartney says that the doctrine of the Virgin Birth "is not a matter of theory and interpretation, but a matter of fact." How does this "doctrine" differ from other statements in our Christian creeds? Do you agree with Macartney's position?
4. Why do you think the Apostle Paul has so little to say regarding the birth of Christ but so much to say about His death?
5. Review Macartney's three main points under "the meaning of the fact." Would you add any to this list?

CHAPTER 2

1. On page 28 Macartney says Christ's fulfillment of prophecy is

"the one great argument of the apostles for the authority of Jesus Christ." Do you consider that important? If so, why?

2. On page 31 Macartney sums up the life of Christ by declaring that "His Incarnation and Death and Resurrection and Ascension and the bestowal by Him of the Holy Spirit were facts that had all been foretold centuries before by the prophets concerning the Christ, and that since Jesus fulfilled these prophecies He must be the Christ; publicly showing by the Scriptures that Jesus was Christ, and that therefore men must obey Him and believe in Him. As Peter put it in his great sermon, 'to him, all prophets bear witness.'" Do you agree with this summation? Is there a category you would add?
3. On page 35 the author says: "Christ forgave the harlot and the extortioner; He forgave Peter who, with cruel oaths denied Him, and the thief on the cross stained with his crimes; but He cannot forgive the man who will not believe." Is this a valid conclusion? If it is, how should it affect your own life? How should it affect the way you work and witness?

CHAPTER 3

1. Another title for this chapter could be, "Was Christ Unique?" Does this clarify its content for you?
2. On page 40 Macartney says, "There is such a thing as truth becoming cold and dead." Do you agree? Can you cite some instances of this fact?
3. On page 41 the author says that one reason Jesus was "an original (i.e., unique) teacher" was "because He was a sinless man," and goes on to expand on the ramifications of this fact. He even calls Jesus a "moral miracle." What does this mean?
4. Also on page 41 he cites the "passive" and "heroic" virtues of Christ. Can you think of others in your acquaintance or circle of friends who exemplify these virtues? Anyone who exemplifies many of them? All? What does such a mental exercise prove to you?
5. Can you think of any more recent leaders who have called on people to follow them? Why is Christ different from any of these?
6. Explore the question, "What is that Gospel?"

CHAPTER 4

1. On page 46 Macartney says, "Christianity cannot be ethically divine and historically false." Explore and discuss that statement.
2. Note the author's definition of a miracle on page 47, and look up other definitions in both secular and biblical dictionaries. Can miracles happen outside the power of God?
3. Discuss the idea that "a miracle is a violation of law, or God as reveals Himself in nature," and the implication "that we can know all about God and His ways" (page 48).
4. On the same page Macartney says: "A God who made a world and then shut Himself out from it so that He could never enter it again, never arrest, regulate, add to its laws of working, would be no God at all." Think about and discuss this concept.
5. Is it possible to believe in Christ without accepting His miracles (see page 52)?
6. Beginning on page 51 Macartney discusses two aspects of "the meaning of the miracles." Reread and discuss the two concepts He expounds.

CHAPTER 5

1. "The two great needs of our fallen and lost humanity are love and forgiveness" (page 55). Is this true? Was it as true in the days of the New Testament?
2. On pages 57 and 58 Macartney lists some of the claims Jesus made for Himself, i.e., omnipotence, infallibility, sinlessness, omnipresence, etc. List these claims and discuss what they mean to you as a Christian, to the Christian church as a whole.
3. Compare Peter's statement to that of the man healed from blindness (page 59).
4. On page 60 Macartney says, "the character of Jesus is humanity's one great moral asset."
5. Look at and list the four great miracles discussed in the latter part of the chapter. How are they different? Similar?
6. Reread the poem on page 62. Discuss its meaning.

CHAPTER 6

1. On page 65 Macartney quotes a church member: "I think we are

saved by obeying the teachings of Jesus, by following His example and doing His will; not by His death." Do you know churches (or people) who feel this way? The author goes on to say: ". . . two kinds of Christianity are being preached and taught in our churches today. One is a Christianity of ideals and inspiration and good works. Christ is preached as the great teacher, example, inspirer and leader. With some He is divine, with others He is only man, though the noblest flower which has bloomed on the stock of our humanity. This is a Christianity of instruction and education. If its disciples use the word 'salvation,' that is all they mean." Do you agree with that description?

2. On page 66 he describes another kind of Christianity: ". . . the Christianity of redemption. Man is a sinner and under the condemnation of God's law. He could do nothing to save himself. But God sent His Only Begotten Son, Jesus Christ, to die for man, in place of man, as a substitute for man. By faith in Christ as Redeemer, man is forgiven, the guilt and the stain of his sin is taken away, and he is restored to the family of God. In the former kind of Christianity, the Christianity of education and ideals and inspiration, the death of Christ is but an incident, though a moving and beautiful one. In the Christianity of redemption the death of Christ is the one grand truth around which gather all the other truths of the Christian religion." Of which persuasion is your church? Or are there both kinds of Christians in your group?
3. Are you convinced by the author's arguments under "the testimony of Peter" as to the character of true Christianity?
4. Compare Peter's teaching to John's (see page 69).
5. Compare their teachings to those of Paul. Do all three agree?
6. In the latter part of the chapter Macartney devotes several pages to a discussion of "the testimony of Jesus" as to the meaning and prominence of His death to the Christian faith. Review each of these four sections and discuss.

CHAPTER 7

1. On page 76 Macartney says: "The church was established in the earth by the Resurrection of Jesus from the dead." Is this an oversimplification? Were there other causes?

2. On page 78 Macartney says: "The belief in the Resurrection created the Church, established it in the world, and has kept it in the world for more than 19 centuries." Is this a valid statement?
3. Under "the evidences for the Resurrection" Macartney lists four "proofs." Review and discuss.

CHAPTER 8

1. On page 85 Macartney says: "There is, today, an ever-increasing tendency to dissociate Christianity from its supernatural facts and to try to take and enjoy its great principles and high hopes without regard to the truth of the alleged facts upon which it must stand." Is this true of a sizable segment of Christendom today?
2. On page 89 the writer says: "The Scriptures do not locate or describe heaven, but when Jesus ascended into heaven to the right hand of God, He passed through into a world that is just as real as the world in which we live today." Does this give us any hints as to heaven's location?
3. On the same page Macartney says: " In that invisible world to which Christ has gone, the great office of our Lord is that of an intercessor with God for all who in this life believe on Him." What does this mean to you as a Christian? Read the rest of the section and discuss.
4. Read the section headed "The Heavenly Possibilities of Human Nature" and discuss.
5. On page 92 the author declares, "but this rejected Christ holds the helm of the universe as He sits at God's right hand." What does this fact mean to you as a Christian?

CHAPTER 9

1. On page 97 Macartney writes: ". . . the abuse of the doctrine (of Christ's coming again) on the one hand, and the total neglect of it on the other, is no reason why Christian believers should not be instructed concerning it, and receive comfort and inspiration from it." Is it possible to discuss the return of Christ without date-setting?
2. On page 98 Macartney says: ". . . the time of His coming is unpredictable and unexpected." What effect should that fact have on Christians? What does it mean to you personally?

3. On page 99 he adds: "If Christ is not coming again, then His moral authority is destroyed and we cannot worship Him as God." What does he mean by this statement? Is it true?
4. On the same page he adds: "To the most careless reader of the New Testament it is evident that the driving power of the apostolic Church was the belief held by those who formed it that Christ was coming back to earth, and the hope that He was coming in their day, before they died." Is the same "driving power" evident today?
5. On page 100 Macartney points out that ". . . most Christians believe that before Christ comes the world must be evangelized." Is that a common feeling today? Is the Church making progress in this campaign?
6. On page 103 Macartney says that a segment of the Church believes "in the inevitable progress of human society toward perfection" but disbelief is not nearly so strong as it once was. Do you agree?
7. Reread his discussion on pages 104 to 106. Do you agree with his conclusions?

CHAPTER 10

1. React to the quote from Dr. Vedder's *The Fundamentals of Christianity* on page 108. Do you agree or disagree?
2. Do you think Paul "added to the teachings of Jesus"? (see page 109).
3. Did Paul's ideas differ from the disciples who walked physically with the Savior—or did he just "see farther"?
4. Macartney (on page 111) says that ". . . to say that Paul differs from Jesus as to the meaning of the Gospel amounts to saying that the Christian Church was a colossal . . . mistake." Is this true?
5. On page 112 Macartney says that Paul's concept of Christ and that of the Gospels is "identical." Do you agree?
6. Compare Paul's teachings to those of Jesus on such matters as personal purity, attitude toward others, etc. Is there a difference?
7. What is the reason, do you think, for the prominence given in the Scriptures to the substitutionary death of Christ?

CHAPTER 11

1. Notice the quotation from a Catholic journal on page 125. Do you think this same mind-set exists in Protestantism?
2. What does Macartney mean by the appellation "another Jesus"? Does a sizable segment of the church today preach and proclaim "another Jesus"?
3. On page 129 Macartney says, "The evidence for His walking *upon* the sea is just the same as the evidence for His walking *by* the sea," and says that critics of the supernatural birth of Christ have a "repugnance for the supernatural as related to Christianity." Think about and discuss the ramifications of that position.
4. On page 130 Macartney writes: "A preacher tells me he cannot 'swallow' the story of Jesus walking on the sea. Very well. But what is he going to do with the Jesus, who, when asked by the messengers of John in prison, 'Art thou he that should come or look we for another?' answered, 'Go and tell John that the lame walk, the deaf hear, the blind see, the lepers are cleansed, the dead are raised up and the poor have the gospel preached unto them'? Even with the recorded miracles deleted, the Gospels still present to us a Jesus who claimed that He worked miracles." Discuss the ramifications of that paragraph.

CHAPTER 12

1. On page 136 Macartney says: "The great question of religion is, whether or not God has spoken to man, and whether or not we have a true record of that revelation." Do you agree? Is this an over simplification?
2. On page 138 says concerning the Virgin Birth: "The modernists are simply saying what the unbelievers of every age have said. The only difference is that Celsus and Paine said it from *outside* the church, whereas the modernist says it from *inside* the church." Is this happening today as well?
3. Review the claims of agnostics quoted in this chapter. Formulate your own answers to their arguments.
4. Macartney seems to conclude that underlying all objections to the significance of the Cross of Christ is man's denial of his sinful state and need of a Savior. Do you agree with his position?